baby food
maker
cookbook

baby food maker cookbook

125 Fresh, Wholesome, Organic Recipes for Your Baby Food Maker Device or Stovetop

PHILIA KELNHOFER

HARMONY BOOKS
NEW YORK

The material in this book is supplied for informational purposes only and is not meant to take the place of your child's pediatrician. No book can replace a trusted health care professional.

Please be certain to consult with your child's doctor before making any decisions that would affect their health, particularly if they suffer from any medical condition or have any symptom that may require treatment.

Library of Congress Cataloging-in-Publication Data
Names: Kelnhofer, Philia, author.
Title: Baby food maker cookbook : 125 fresh, wholesome, organic recipes for your baby food maker device or stovetop / Philia Kelnhofer.
Description: New York, NY : Harmony Books, [2019]
Identifiers: LCCN 2018046443| ISBN 9781984824578 (trade pbk.) | ISBN 9781984824585 (eISBN)
Subjects: LCSH: Baby foods. | Infants—Nutrition. | LCGFT: Cookbooks.
Classification: LCC TX740 .K457 2019 | DDC 641.3/00832—dc23 LC record available at https://lccn.loc.gov/2018046443

ISBN 978-1-9848-2457-8
Ebook ISBN 978-1-9848-2458-5

Printed in the United States of America

Cover and interior design by Jan Derevjanik
Cover and interior photography by Philia Kelnhofer

10 9 8 7 6 5 4 3 2 1

First Edition

This book is dedicated to all the parents out there feeding their little ones homemade baby food. I know it isn't always easy. You rock.

And to my loves: my husband, Nick, and our son, Benedikt, the best taste testers around. You inspire me to create delicious food.

contents

note from the author 9

introduction 13

block one
single ingredient purees
28

block two
combination purees
50

block three
chunky purees
88

block four
starting solids
136

block five
beyond baby
178

the top 12 ways to use your baby food
maker after baby food 212

appendix: cooking-time guide 220
acknowledgments 222
index 223

If you're reading this book, chances are you have a little one who is ready to start eating, and you're wondering if you should make your baby's food from scratch. Chances are you're also a busy mom who barely has time to brush her hair, so you may be thinking to yourself, "Do I *really* have time to make baby food? On top of diapers and laundry and all the other tedious tasks my bundle of joy brought into my life?"

The answer is a big, wholehearted YES.

Making baby food is actually really easy. Whether you're using a baby food maker device or the stovetop plus a blender (this cookbook works for either setup), it's not some insurmountable task that will take hours out of your day. And the benefits are big: You'll know what you're feeding your baby, you'll save money making your baby food, and, if you're like me, you'll feel a sense of pride for providing the best for your baby.

This is true whether you consider yourself a cook or not, as long as you're equipped with the right information. Now, I've always loved cooking; I even write a food blog (sweetphi.com) where I share easy recipes for busy people. So I was very excited when my pediatrician said I could start feeding my son real food at 4 months. Naturally I envisioned myself whipping up wholesome, nourishing purees for him, easy-peasy.

Things did not go exactly as I thought they would.

After doing some research, I had decided that my son's first food would be sweet potatoes. There's no hard-and-fast rule about what your baby's first bite should be, but I wanted a fruit or vegetable that would be smooth and creamy and mild, while packing in some great nutrition—and sweet potatoes, with their beta-carotene, vitamin C, fiber, and potassium, fit the bill. So I bought an organic sweet potato (only the best

for my baby's first bites!), wrapped it up in aluminum foil so that the edges wouldn't get crispy, and put it in the oven to bake. Because that's what you do with sweet potatoes. You bake them. Right?

After an hour, I checked on the potato. It wasn't cooked through, so back into the oven it went. Half an hour later, I removed it from the oven and let it cool so I could touch it. Then I peeled it, then I blended it with some water, and *finally*, after two hours, I had some sweet potato puree that I could feed my son.

The joy on his face when he tasted his first little spoonful of food—that moment is something I will never forget.

Then for the next few days he had a few small bites of sweet potato puree. But on day three or four, I smelled the sweet potato before feeding it to him and it had gone bad! After spending over two hours making the food only for it to go to waste so soon, preparing baby food just didn't seem like it would be worth it.

I had so many questions: Does all baby food take that long to make? Am I doing it wrong? What quantities should I make? How do I warm food? How do I freeze food? How long is it good for?

It seemed daunting.

So I went to the store to buy some premade baby food.

The colorful packaging and different flavor combinations looked great. I got home, squeezed some out into a little bowl, and stopped short. It was brown. Why was it brown? Colorful fruits and veggies like carrots, apples, and beets are all very vibrant in color. But these store-bought baby foods, no matter how fresh and organic their marketing makes them sound, are processed and filled with preservatives that keep them shelf-stable. The baby food you find at the store is probably older than your baby.

Back to attempting to make baby food I went.

For my next foray into baby food from scratch, I used the stovetop and a blender, and found myself snitching bites because the combinations tasted so good. To this day, I make this amazing apple pear cinnamon sauce for my son . . . and for my husband and me to snack on either solo or added to yogurt and granola parfaits (see page 183).

Then someone told me about this new device: the baby food maker. I really wanted to dislike it. I said to myself, "Another kitchen appliance? Am I even going to use it? How good can it really be?"

I purchased one and made a batch of Sweet Potato Puree (page 32). This time my experience making baby food was amazing. All I did was peel the sweet potato, cut it into cubes, add water to the reservoir, and hit a button. I literally walked away and came back 25 minutes later when the timer went off. I blended it and boom: sweet potato puree for my baby.

It was so easy. Honestly, it was life changing.

A baby food maker makes baby food with minimal involvement, and it is so incredibly easy to use. I could not (and cannot, to this day) stop raving about it to anyone who will listen.

There was a problem, though. I was free-forming my own baby foods based on what I knew about best first foods and the device's instruction manual (sometimes only in a foreign language). There wasn't a cookbook available showing everything you can do with a baby food maker. I would tell my new mom friends how amazing the baby food maker is, and they would ask for recipes. That's how this book came to be.

These 125 recipes are everything you need to know to make nutritious and delicious wholesome food for your baby, from the first bite. For those who don't want to spend hours upon hours trying to search for recipes or how-tos or experimenting in the kitchen, this book is for you. First read through the next pages for general information about using your baby food maker device, buying ingredients, and storing foods safely, and general first-food guidelines. I've also included a handy chart for tracking your baby's introduction to foods in those first months; keep notes on those pages as you work through these recipes.

During the process of using a baby food maker, I've fallen so in love with the device that I've even made recipes that adults will enjoy as well. Seriously, try the Edamame Dip on page 189 or the Chickpea–Sweet Potato Spread (page 187). They are as good to eat as they are easy to whip up as well as great for entertaining, and your little one can enjoy bites of it too!

Looking for even more recipes and inspiration? I've included many how-to tutorials and additional resources and recipes online at sweetphi.com/extras.

I hope you and your little one enjoy.

—PHI

introduction

HOW TO USE THIS BOOK

My hope is that this book is a helpful resource to you. The recipes on the following pages are broken down into single ingredient purees, combination ingredient purees, purees that can be a little chunkier, starting solids recipes, and then a few recipes for adults. I like to think of these purees as building blocks—you start with some basics, and then add them together, and then add spices and textures. There isn't any strict timeline you need to follow, as every baby is different; you can find readiness guidelines on pages 15–17 and a chart to track your introduction of ingredients on pages 26–27. And these recipes aren't just for baby! I've included ways to adapt some recipes for adults; many of the recipes can be dips, spreads, soups, or even whole meals. Plus I've included a whole section at the end devoted to post-baby uses for the device.

I did this because I'm a firm believer in making use of the appliances you buy. Nothing makes me sadder than the sight of an old device collecting dust on the kitchen counter. Luckily, there are amazing ways to use a baby food maker well beyond the baby years, and this book will show you how the small size, speed, and ease of the device can be just what you need in a pinch—much easier than firing up the stovetop. Need a quick side dish for that steak you're grilling? Make a batch of Sweet Potato Puree (page 32). Have friends coming over? I'd highly recommend the Sun-Dried Tomato Spread (page 200) or the spicy Edamame Dip (page 189). Or craving a little dessert on a busy night? Make the Cheaters' Berry Crumble on page 184. Want to take your pancakes or waffles to the next level? Add some Strawberry Sauce (page 190).

But many of you are busy parents hoping to nourish your baby with the most wholesome, real foods possible. This book is your complete guide to your baby's first meals. Introducing your baby to solid foods is such a huge milestone in life. Here are the resources and recipes to guide you along your journey of making food for your baby.

WHY MAKE YOUR OWN BABY FOOD?

Making your own baby food can seem a little daunting, but I promise you, it's actually quite simple. And there are many reasons why you should make your own baby food! Here are my top six reasons.

You can choose the best ingredients. I recommend choosing fresh, local, seasonal, and organic when possible. But let's face it, that's not always possible. How am I supposed to buy fresh mango in the state of Wisconsin in December? Sometimes buying a bag of frozen organic mango is the only option, and, honestly, it's just as good! I would recommend frozen organic ingredients over fresh conventional ones.

There are no funky ingredients or preservatives. When I first started trying to make my son's food, I didn't know what I was doing. I failed pretty miserably (see the story on page 9, when I spent over two hours trying to make sweet potato puree). So I turned to store-bought food. Some of it was completely fine, but sometimes my son would get a little rash all over his tummy and chest. Our pediatrician told us to bring in everything he was eating, because nothing else new was being introduced. After carefully examining the labels, the culprit was citric acid—a perfectly safe preservative, but one to which my son was sensitive. When you're making baby food from scratch, you know exactly what you're putting in it!

You save money. Like a lot of money—I'm talking dollars per batch. For example, I figured that organic sweet potatoes cost $0.13 per ounce. A 3-ounce pouch of premade organic sweet potatoes costs $1.20. That's a $0.27 cost difference per ounce; the store-bought pouch is about triple the cost of the homemade version. All the data I've come across estimates that making homemade baby food saves at least 60 percent.

It's super convenient. When you're making baby food at home, all you need is a baby food maker or a pot and a blender (or food processor), and a storage container, reusable pouch, or ice cube tray. You can whip up a batch of baby food anytime, even with ingredients you might already have on hand! It takes less than half an hour, start to finish.

Homemade tastes better than store-bought. Homemade baby food is tasty and really lets your baby experience how food is supposed to taste and feel. Store-bought baby food just doesn't have that same taste.

You're raising an adventurous eater. Studies have shown that early exposure to different flavors and textures promotes having a more adventurous palate and varied diet later on. Store-bought pouches have a more limited range of textures and flavors than you'll create in your kitchen!

WHAT ARE BABY FOOD MAKERS AND HOW TO USE THEM

Baby food makers are devices that both steam and puree, an all-in-one baby food–making device. They're not just a smaller blender or food processor. Baby food makers have a heating and steaming mechanism that cooks food, and then a blending mechanism that purees the cooked food. The recipes in this book work for the two types of baby food maker devices (described below) that I've come across with slightly different instructions. Each recipe will include instructions for the "water level" and "fillable tank" types of devices, as well as instructions for the stovetop plus blender/food processor.

Water Level Devices: This type has two parts: (1) a steamer basket where you deposit the food and (2) a water tank or reservoir that you fill with water; the level of water depends on what is being cooked. The water steams the food, and when the food is done cooking, you pour the food from the steamer basket into the blending bowl, which has a blade it in, and then you blend the food. There is one button you press to steam and a knob you turn to blend. You may come across a water level device that does not include a steamer basket (that's why you'll see that the recipes direct you to put ingredients in the steamer basket or cooking compartment; if you don't have a steamer basket, just put the food in whatever cooking compartment your device has). All recipes will work for both types of water level devices except the handful in Block Five: Beyond Baby that require a steamer basket. Those recipes are clearly marked as Water Level Device with Steamer Basket recipes. *Brands include* Béaba Babycook, QOOC Mini Baby Food Maker.

Fillable Tank Devices: This type of baby food maker does it all in one compartment—it doesn't have a basket. You put the food into the compartment (that has blades at the bottom) and water in the water tank. The water tank just needs to be full; you don't need to pour it to different levels depending on what you're cooking. This type of baby food maker has a cook-time function and blend function that needs to be programmed prior to cooking, and then the cooking and blending happen in that same compartment. *Brands include* Baby Brezza One-Step Baby Food Maker, Babymoov Nutribaby Baby Food Maker.

Both types of baby food makers are great. They are set-it-and-forget-it type of machines, usually with only 5 minutes of prep time, and the longest cook time you'll encounter is 25 minutes. You fill the machine with water, put the food you're cooking into the machine, and press one button or program it, and you're done.

If you have the water-level type of baby food maker, you can put a little ramekin in the steamer basket and make dishes like the baby Banana Bread on page 205, or the Chocolate Cakelette on page 210. But never fear, the vast majority of recipes in this book work for the full range of baby food maker devices.

I've included instructions on how to make baby food with both types of baby food makers in each recipe, and if you do not have a baby food maker, I've included easy instructions for preparing the recipes on the stovetop plus a blender. I recommend using a high-powered blender or a food processor. Cuisinart is a great food processor; Dash, Vitamix, and Blendtec all make great blenders.

There are no yields in this book as you'd normally find in a cookbook, because the amount your baby eats is extremely variable. Ingredient quantities are also more flexible than in many cookbooks, so you don't have to worry about finding, for example, a small, medium, or large-sized apple. When your baby is first eating solids, they're having about a teaspoon a day, and a good amount may end up on their face and high chair. Store what's left for a future meal; you can find information about storing and freezing baby food on page 18 of this introduction, and recipes will include information about storability.

BUYING ORGANIC, LOCAL, AND SEASONAL INGREDIENTS

When possible, organic ingredients are best to use. And organic, local, and seasonal ingredients are even better to use. Not only are you supporting your community by buying local, but the nutritional makeup of the ingredients is better.

Have you ever wondered why a summer tomato or fall apple purchased at a local farmers' market tastes so much better than their counterparts purchased off season at the grocery store? It's because fruit and vegetables not grown locally are typically picked prematurely, which arrests the development of nutrients, and then flown in to your grocery store. These fruits and vegetables are also treated with special gases to slow the ripening process, further depleting their nutritional composition.

Since 2004, the Environmental Working Group (ewg.org) has published lists of the "Dirty Dozen" and "Clean Fifteen" every year, laying out which produce has the highest and lowest concentration of pesticide residue. If you're wondering where to spend your dollars on organic produce, I would recommend purchasing fruits and vegetables on the Dirty Dozen list as organic, and perhaps not worrying as much about the Clean Fifteen.

While it is preferable to use organic, local, and seasonal ingredients, it is not always an option. I live in the state of Wisconsin, so in the summertime I have easy access to farmers' markets and buy organic ingredients, especially those on the Dirty Dozen list, whenever I can. But in the winter? Not so much. I say go with the best you can find available. I also love relying on frozen organic vegetables when I cannot find the fresh version.

GENERAL FEEDING READINESS GUIDELINES

It is important to remember that every baby is different. There is no hard-and-fast rule that when your baby reaches 6 months of age they will be ready to start solid food. Typically, infants are ready to begin exploring food anywhere between 4 and

the dirty dozen

*produce with the highest
amount of pesticide residues*

- Strawberries
- Spinach
- Nectarines
- Apples
- Grapes
- Peaches
- Cherries
- Pears
- Tomatoes
- Celery
- Potatoes
- Sweet bell peppers

the clean fifteen

*produce less likely to
contain pesticide residues*

- Avocados
- Sweet corn
- Pineapples
- Cabbages
- Onions
- Frozen sweet peas
- Papayas
- Asparagus
- Mangoes
- Eggplants
- Honeydews
- Kiwis
- Cantaloupes
- Cauliflower
- Broccoli

6 months, and the American Academy of Pediatrics[*] recommends the introduction of solid foods at that time. But they suggest following developmental progress rather than age to determine readiness.

Their guidelines to help assess your baby's readiness to accept solid food[†] include the following:

- **Head control:** Your baby has good head control, meaning he or she can keep their head in an upright position, unassisted.

- **Sitting supported:** Your baby is able to sit in a high chair, feeding seat, or infant seat, supported, in order to sit upright to swallow.

- **Curiosity:** The infant opens his or her mouth when food comes their way. He or she may watch others eat, reach for food, and seem eager to be fed.

- **Ability to swallow:** The infant can move food from a spoon into his or her throat. Your baby's mouth and tongue develop in sync with his or her digestive system. To start solids, babies should be able to move food to the back of their mouths and swallow it, instead of using their tongues to push food out of their mouths.

- **Weight:** Your baby has doubled his or her birth weight.

So once your baby has hit these five benchmarks, you're ready to feed him or her for the first time! You'll want to start with a simple puree and keep track of the ingredients you introduce (one at a time, a few days apart) in the chart on pages 26–27. Here are some tips to keep in mind as you plan to feed your baby for the first time, and then I'll go over general instructions for making, freezing, and storing purees, followed by guidelines for progressing to more complex foods.

FEEDING TIPS

Use ripe or almost ripe produce. Even when produce looks ripe and you could probably blend it with no cooking required, I suggest steaming it a little. Just a few minutes of cooking makes the produce perfect for blending and creates a smooth, silky texture.

Use frozen produce. If you are running low on time and don't feel like peeling and chopping, check the freezer section. There are so many wonderful pre-peeled and chopped fruits and vegetables (think mangoes, cherries, peas, green beans, corn, etc.).

Think small. When you're first starting to feed baby, only a small amount of food will be eaten. They usually eat between 1 and 2 teaspoons, once a day! Freeze the rest of the food that they don't eat (most purees are good for up to 2 months in the freezer; see page 18 for more instructions).

Start the meal with breast milk or formula. Before you start feeding them, you want to give them a little feeding of breast milk or formula—not a full feeding, but a partial one. If baby normally eats 6 ounces, give baby 3. You want baby not to be too hungry, not too full, but content.

One ingredient at a time. When you first introduce food, introduce one new ingredient at a time, and stick with that single ingredient for a few days (4 to 7 days) before moving on to a new one. It sometimes takes a few days for a rash or other signs of an allergy or irritation to present itself, so you want to make sure that baby reacts well to each new food. Use the chart on pages 26–27 to track the ingredients they've been given and take notes about how they react!

Build on ingredients you've already introduced. You can keep giving them foods they've already tried as you introduce new foods one at a time. That way you can rule out sensitivity to any new ingredients while increasing the diversity of what your baby eats. That is why you go from single ingredient purees to combination purees, and then add in spices and herbs.

[*] "Infant Food and Feeding," American Academy of Pediatrics, accessed October 2, 2018, aap.org/en-us/advocacy-and-policy /aap-health-initiatives/HALF-implementation-Guide/Age-Specific -Content/Pages/Infant-Food-and-Feeding.aspx.
[†] "Bite-Sized Milestones: Signs of Solid Food Readiness," Healthy Children.org, last updated January 16, 2018, healthychildren.org /English/ages-stages/baby/feeding-nutrition/Pages Bite-Sized -Milestones-Signs-of-Solid-Food-Readiness-aspx.

It's going to get messy. Don't rush to wipe away the mess at the first sign of it. The mess is part of the fun, so don't stress about it.

Enjoy! At first it's all about exploring new tastes and textures, so go slow and enjoy this huge milestone of introducing your baby to solids!

HOW TO MAKE AND FREEZE PUREES

Making baby food can be broken down into six simple steps:

1. **Prepping.** Make sure to wash, peel, and chop fresh fruits and vegetables. Do not use fresh or frozen food that contains added sugars, sauces, or flavorings. When cooking meat, be sure to remove any fat, skin, or bones before cooking.

2. **Cooking.** Cook food properly by steaming it in your baby food maker or on the stovetop. Fruit and vegetables are done when they can easily be pierced or mashed with a fork. Meat is done when cooked to the appropriate temperature. Beef and pork should be cooked to an internal temperature of 145°F, and poultry to 165°F.

3. **Blending.** Blend food in a baby food maker or in a blender or food processor. If the puree is too thick, add a little liquid to reach the desired consistency (you can use breast milk, formula, or water).

4. **Serving.** Serve cooked food immediately after it has cooled a little, or store it in an airtight container or reusable storage pouch for no more than 3 days for fruits and vegetables, and no more than 24 hours for meats, poultry, fish, and egg yolk. Or freeze it.

5. **Storing and freezing.** To freeze food, make your puree of choice and then pour it into a clean and appropriately sanitized ice cube tray (sanitize by cleaning in hot soapy water as you normally would) or a divided silicone tray; I like the silicone trays the best because the cubes come out the easiest. Once frozen, cubes of food should be transferred to a freezer-safe resealable plastic bag. Always date and label the contents of the bag. Food can be stored safely in the freezer for up to 2 months. Each

cube of food should equal approximately 1 ounce (2 tablespoons) of puree. Defrost frozen baby food via the baby food maker, microwave, stovetop, or refrigerator, and use within 48 hours of thawing.

6. **Thawing.** To thaw baby food you have four options.

   a. **Baby Food Maker.** Take a puree cube (or cubes) out of the freezer bag and place in the blending bowl. Add water to water level 2 or 10 minutes, and blend when the timer goes off.

   b. **Microwave.** Take a puree cube (or cubes) out of the freezer bag and place in a microwave-safe container. Microwave in 20-second increments, stirring in between, until thawed.

   c. **Stovetop.** Take a puree cube (or cubes) out of the freezer, place in a small 2-quart saucepan, and cook over medium-high heat, stirring occasionally, until thawed.

   d. **Fridge.** Take a puree cube (or cubes) out of the freezer, put into a small storage container, and let it thaw in the refrigerator. This method takes the longest, usually 12 to 24 hours.

You don't want to overdo it with batch cooking, though. Listen, I know the allure of spending a day making one puree after another and freezing them for a later time. I tried that once. I had a whole game plan where I bought fruits and vegetables and had my baby food maker and stovetop going nonstop. I made fifteen different purees. Different purees! It was enough for a few months' supply.

But when I defrosted them, they just weren't the same. Some fruit and vegetable blends separated when thawing. Then I had some in the freezer for 3 months before they were needed, and upon trying a little spoon before feeding it to my son, I just couldn't go through with it and feed it to him. It tasted weird, like it had freezer burn! In my experience, I have found that pureed food lasts for up to 2 months in the freezer. Beyond that, it starts getting a weird "freezer taste" to it.

That is why I advise against overdoing it with batch cooking.

Also, when your baby is first starting out, they're eating about a teaspoon a day. That's it! One sweet potato will last you weeks with some of it in the fridge and most of it in the freezer. It's so easy to make more food than you need.

Plus, with a baby food maker, you'll find that making the food is so easy and quick that you won't need to stockpile and make food ahead.

HOW TO TRANSITION FROM PUREES TO SOLIDS

It's been amazing to watch my son, Ben, go from eating a few tiny drippy spoonfuls of puree to reaching for baby meatballs (see page 143) to picking up pieces of food himself. When I was first starting to feed him, I wondered how much food I should be feeding him and how many times per day. While every baby is different, here are some general feeding guidelines:

- **4 to 6 months:** single ingredient purees, very liquidy and smooth, 1 teaspoon to 2 tablespoons per feeding, 1 feeding per day

- **6 to 7 months:** combination ingredient purees, don't need to be as liquidy but should still be smooth, 2 to 4 tablespoons per feeding, 1 or 2 feedings per day

- **7 to 9 months:** combination ingredient purees, chunkier purees but still primarily smooth and blended, introducing herbs and spices, proteins, and grains, ¼ to ½ cup, 2 or 3 feedings per day

- **9 to 12 months:** chunkier purees as well as small, softer solids and things that can be broken up, mashed with a fork, and picked up by baby, ½ cup to 1 cup food at meals, 3 feedings per day plus a snack (can give smaller portions of steamed veggies at snacks—sweet potatoes, peaches, mangoes, and carrots). Once baby starts trying to pick up the food from the spoon (i.e., their pincer grip has developed and they can move food into their own mouths) or they can easily mush food with their gums, you know it's time for these chunkier purees and softer solids!

In this book, the stages are organized as blocks of time that build from one to the next. Block One is single ingredient purees; Block Two is combination purees; Block Three adds texture, herbs, spices, proteins, and grains; and Block Four is chunkier purees and soft solids.

Once your baby starts developing their pincer grip, tries to grab the food off the spoon, and can eat chunkier purees without a problem, it's a good sign they are ready for softer solids and food that can be broken up/mashed with a fork.

A FEW NOTES ON FOOD ALLERGIES

A true food allergy is a potentially life-threatening reaction that can occur within minutes or seconds after exposure to the allergen and requires an injection of epinephrine and a trip to the emergency room. Please always discuss allergy concerns with your pediatrician. If you are aware of a close relative (parents, siblings) with a true food allergy, consult your doctor to make a plan on how to introduce those foods; generally, the literature says not to introduce them before 12 months.

The Food Allergen Labeling and Consumer Protection Act, with guidance from the Food and Drug Administration (FDA), lists these as the most common allergens:

• Eggs

• Fish

• Milk

• Peanuts

• Shellfish

• Soy

• Tree nuts (such as almonds, cashews, walnuts)

• Wheat

A food allergy can be a very serious issue. That's why you want to introduce one food at a time over the course of several days, because sometimes it takes a few minutes or hours after consumption for a food allergy reaction to present itself. Some signs to look out for are rash, hives, vomiting, diarrhea, teary eyes, face or tongue swelling, or difficulty breathing within a few hours of consuming food. If you notice any of these, discontinue food use immediately and discuss the situation with your pediatrician.

A food intolerance is different than a true allergy. My son was very sensitive to citric acid, a perfectly safe preservative used in store-bought baby food. Every time I gave him food that contained citric acid, he would get a little rash on his tummy and chest. We took him to the pediatrician immediately and were able to figure out the cause because the only thing we had done differently was feed him solids. He was fine when he had homemade sweet potato puree, but the jarred stuff with the preservative irritated him, so it was an easy decision for me to make his baby food. He has since outgrown his intolerance, but it's still best to be careful and always discuss concerns with your pediatrician.

SUBSTITUTIONS IN RECIPES

Recipes are meant to be customized to your individual tastes and based on what you have on hand. Don't have any butternut squash? Not a problem, you can swap in sweet potatoes. Is your baby going through a phase where they don't like eggs? Try switching to tofu. Here are some common substitutes I use:

• **Apple:** pear

• **Beef:** lamb

• **Cherries:** cranberries

• **Chicken:** turkey, pork, tofu

• **Eggs:** tofu

• **1 tablespoon fresh herbs:** 1 teaspoon dried herbs

• **Leeks:** onions

• **Quinoa:** brown rice

• **Spinach:** Swiss chard, kale

• **Sweet potato:** butternut squash, pumpkin

SPICES AND HERBS

Herbs and spices are a fantastic way for baby to develop his or her palate. Not only do they add flavor but they also add nutrients.

Fresh herbs with more tender leaves, like basil, cilantro, and parsley, tend to work better when added after food has been cooked, while woody stemmed herbs, such as rosemary and thyme, withstand heat well, so they can be added at the beginning of cooking.

Dried herbs can be used in place of fresh herbs. Since dried herbs are more concentrated, you need less of them. If a recipe calls for 1 tablespoon of fresh herbs, use 1 teaspoon dried herbs. The conversion factor is generally three parts fresh to one part dried (since there are 3 teaspoons in 1 tablespoon).

Herbs and spices are a fantastic way to introduce baby to the flavors of different cultures as well. There are innumerable flavor combinations. Here I've listed some of my favorite ways to combine herbs and spices with foods:

- **Allspice or cinnamon:** apples, bananas, pears, pumpkin, sweet potatoes, butternut squash, oatmeal, yogurt, beef, chicken

- **Cumin:** carrots, sweet potatoes, tomatoes, beans, grains, beef, chicken, lamb

- **Garlic:** broccoli, cauliflower, zucchini, quinoa, all meats, tofu

- **Ginger:** apples, carrots, peaches, pears, squash, sweet potatoes, quinoa, all meats, tofu

- **Nutmeg:** apples, carrots, pumpkin, grains

- **Onion:** any vegetable, beans, all meats, tofu

- **Oregano:** potatoes, beans, grains, all meats and fish, tofu

- **Rosemary:** potatoes, beans, grains, all meats and fish, tofu

- **Thyme:** potatoes, beans, grains, all meats and fish, tofu

- **Turmeric:** carrots, sweet potatoes, beans, grains, chicken

Time Saving Trick: Use garlic powder for flavoring if you don't have fresh garlic cloves (just be careful not to add garlic salt as a baby's kidneys cannot handle too much salt).

BABY'S PREFERENCES AND TRYING NEW FOODS

Before I started feeding Ben his first foods, I wondered, "Will I know what he likes and doesn't like?" Now I know that babies don't leave us in the dark about their preferences. After introducing different foods and combinations, your baby will definitely let you know what they like and what they don't like.

But their preferences will also change frequently.

They might gobble something up one day, and then spit it out the next.

On average, a baby needs to try a food ten to twelve times before they will get used to it. So please don't write off a food if your baby doesn't seem to like it the first time you offer it. Try again in a few days, or even try with a different texture or combination. For example, when I first gave my baby beans, he made a face that was admittedly pretty funny but that also led me to believe he didn't want anything to do with beans. I then tried beans mixed with avocado, a food I knew he loved (see the Beef, Avocado, and Black Bean Puree on page 116). He ate the puree right up. Now he eats black beans on their own and loves them, so it's all about trying things over and over again and in different ways.

My mother shares a similar story about me. When I was just starting out with food, I apparently wanted nothing to do with apples. She said she tried a different variety of apples, thinking some were sweeter than others, but still I wouldn't touch apples. Any time apples came near my mouth, I'd turn my head away and spit them out. One day when she was making something with cherries, she decided to give me some cherries with apples, and that I ate. Nowadays, I love apples. In fact, one of my favorite recipes in this book is the apple pear cinnamon puree that I use in yogurt parfaits on page 183. It's a common breakfast and snack recipe in my house.

It's all about trying things over again and in different combinations, so please don't write a food off until you've given it several tries. Also, babies look at your reaction, so don't get frustrated! Try to have fun with this process of exploration!

MAKE IT FUN

I can tell you firsthand that feeding a baby is not always the cleanest endeavor. Don't stress! Bibs, a good washcloth, and a fun outlook can make all the difference in the world. Grab your phone to take some pictures! For years to come you can look back and laugh at the mess that was made. When my son started eating, I snapped a quick picture with my phone. The excitement in his eyes when he tried his first bites of real food is so special to remember. The first time he tried plums (Plum Puree, page 47), the deep red color was on everything! It was a beautiful mess. I'm happy to report the stains came out in the wash.

One of my friends would strip her baby down to the diaper and set up an elaborate tarp under the highchair because she didn't want a mess. After a week of this setup, she realized she was spending more time trying to contain the mess than she would if she just cleaned up after the fact. Now we share funny photos of baby mess.

THE DOS AND DON'TS OF MAKING BABY FOOD AND FEEDING BABIES

There are certain things to keep in mind when making food and feeding babies. Here are some dos and don'ts that may be used for quick reference:

Dos

• Practice appropriate food safety when preparing food: wash your hands, wash utensils used to make food, and avoid cross-contamination.

• Discard any uneaten, leftover food in the infant's dish.

• Determine appropriate textures for your baby's age and development (for example, when to move on to chunkier purees and solids).

• Check the food for temperature, making sure it's not too hot.

• Taste the food; if I'm thawing food, I always make sure it still tastes like it's supposed to.

• Consult with your pediatrician if you have any feeding concerns (like a family history of allergies).

Don'ts

• Don't add salt to baby food; use herbs and spices instead.

• Never use raw honey; it should not be served to infants because of the risk of infant botulism.

• Never thaw food at room temperature; always use one of the methods listed on page 18 (baby food maker, microwave, stovetop, or refrigerator).

• Don't reheat a meal more than once.

• Don't store leftovers from a meal or food that has been in contact with saliva, as it may be contaminated with bacteria. Just throw it away. Also, it is always best to use a clean spoon to add a little food into a clean dish that you feed to baby.

• Don't refreeze baby food that has been removed from the freezer and allowed to thaw already.

• Don't overthink it—your baby is exploring!

HELPFUL TOOLS

Really, all you need to make baby food is a knife, a cutting board, a pot, and some way to puree the food (whether a food processor or a blender), but some other tools will make the process a bit faster and easier. You might want to make sure you use BPA-free tools in your kitchen. (An industrial compound that is often used in plastic containers, bisphenol A—BPA—may seep into food or beverages stored in containers that are made with it.) A baby food maker has made the process of making baby food so much easier, and here are a couple others you might want to have on hand:

- **Vegetable peeler.** Purees made for babies just starting out with food use peeled vegetables to keep the consistency smooth. A vegetable peeler makes the peeling process so much easier. I have two and use them constantly.

- **Knives.** Sharp knives are a must for any kitchen. They make the tedious task of chopping easy-peasy. Two knives are most helpful when making baby food: a chef's knife (or a knife for chopping and cubing) and a paring knife (to core all those fruits and veggies).

- **Cutting board.** You want a nice cutting board to chop all those fruit and veggies on.

- **Colander.** To wash those fruits and veggies clean for baby!

- **Meat thermometer.** You want internal temperature of beef and pork to reach 145°F, and poultry should be 165°F when cooking for babies. I have never had a problem with meat not being cooked through when using the highest setting in my baby food makers.

- **Ice cube trays.** For freezing pureed foods, ice cube trays are great. I recently found some silicone ice cube trays, and those make popping the pureed cubes out super easy.

- **Reusable storage pouches.** If you're looking for a convenient storage system for your baby food, reusable storage pouches are a great option. You can store homemade baby food in them, and when the food is gone, you can clean and reuse them. They're also great for taking baby food on the go.

- **Storage bags.** After the pureed baby food has been frozen in an ice cube tray, store the cubes in a resealable storage bag in the freezer.

- **Spatula.** Scraping food out of a blending bowl is super easy with the help of a spatula.

- **Baby spoons.** Baby spoons are definitely helpful when feeding baby since metal spoons can be a little tough on their gums. They make all sorts of spoons; some are even temperature sensitive and change color if the food is too hot. Whatever type you have will be fine.

HOW THIS BOOK IS STRUCTURED

Each recipe in this book has directions in three columns for baby food makers with water levels (Béaba Babycook; QOOC Mini Baby Food Maker), labeled "Water Level;" baby food makers with a fillable tank (Baby Brezza One-Step Baby Food Maker; Babymoov Nutribaby Baby Food Maker), labeled "Fillable Tank;" and stovetop plus blender or food processor, labeled "Stovetop."

CALENDAR OF FOOD INTRODUCTION

This calendar of food introduction is meant as a guide. Feel free to follow it, or mix it up, modifying it to go at your pace and for the purees you'd like to serve your little one. Want to start with apples instead of sweet potatoes? Do so!

This guide introduces a new food every 4 days. If you'd like to only introduce a new food every week because it's easier to remember, definitely do that.

The general rule is that you want to give the same food for 3 or 4 days to make sure your baby tolerates it before introducing something new.

Below is a sample food introduction calendar, showing how it might look after you've filled yours in; after that are two blank calendars. Use the blank calendars to fill in food introduction and any notes.

sunday	monday	tuesday	wednesday	thursday	friday	saturday
Sweet Potato Puree (page 32)	Sweet Potato Puree (page 32)	Sweet Potato Puree (page 32)	Sweet Potato Puree (page 32)	Apple Puree (page 31)	Apple Puree (page 31)	Apple Puree (page 31)
Apple Puree (page 31)	Carrot Puree (page 35)	Carrot Puree (page 35)	Carrot Puree (page 35)	Carrot Puree (page 35)	Pear Puree (page 40)	Pear Puree (page 40)
Pear Puree (page 40)	Pear Puree (page 40)	Butternut or Acorn Squash Puree (page 37)	Butternut or Acorn Squash Puree (page 37)	Butternut or Acorn Squash Puree (page 37)	Butternut or Acorn Squash Puree (page 37)	Banana Puree (page 42)
Banana Puree (page 42)	Banana Puree (page 42)	Banana Puree (page 42)	Pumpkin Puree (page 38)	Pumpkin Puree (page 38)	Pumpkin Puree (page 38)	Pumpkin Puree (page 38)
Avocado Puree (page 48)	Avocado Puree (page 48)	Avocado Puree (page 48)				

sunday	monday	tuesday	wednesday	thursday	friday	saturday
Pea Puree (page 41)	Pea Puree (page 41)	Pea Puree (page 41)	Pea Puree (page 41)	Broccoli Puree (page 45)	Broccoli Puree (page 45)	Broccoli Puree (page 45)
Broccoli Puree (page 45)	Mango Puree (page 44)	Mango Puree (page 44)	Mango Puree (page 44)	Mango Puree (page 44)	Apple, Corn, and Sweet Potato Puree (page 60)	Apple, Corn, and Sweet Potato Puree (page 60)
Apple, Corn, and Sweet Potato Puree (page 60)	Apple, Corn, and Sweet Potato Puree (page 60)	Apricot, Winter Squash, and Banana Puree (page 62)	Apricot, Winter Squash, and Banana Puree (page 62)	Apricot, Winter Squash, and Banana Puree (page 62)	Apricot, Winter Squash, and Banana Puree (page 62)	Broccoli, Mango, and Zucchini Puree (page 74)
Broccoli, Mango, and Zucchini Puree (page 74)	Broccoli, Mango, and Zucchini Puree (page 74)	Broccoli, Mango, and Zucchini Puree (page 74)	Bell Pepper and Sweet Potato Puree (page 67)	Bell Pepper and Sweet Potato Puree (page 67)	Bell Pepper and Sweet Potato Puree (page 67)	Bell Pepper and Sweet Potato Puree (page 67)
Mango, Pineapple, and Pumpkin Puree (page 83)	Mango, Pineapple, and Pumpkin Puree (page 83)	Mango, Pineapple, and Pumpkin Puree (page 83)				

sunday	monday	tuesday	wednesday	thursday	friday	saturday
food:	food:	food:	food:	food:	food:	food:
notes:	notes:	notes:	notes:	notes:	notes:	notes:
food:	food:	food:	food:	food:	food:	food:
notes:	notes:	notes:	notes:	notes:	notes:	notes:
food:	food:	food:	food:	food:	food:	food:
notes:	notes:	notes:	notes:	notes:	notes:	notes:
food:	food:	food:	food:	food:	food:	food:
notes:	notes:	notes:	notes:	notes:	notes:	notes:
food:	food:	food:	food:	food:	food:	food:
notes:	notes:	notes:	notes:	notes:	notes:	notes:

sunday	monday	tuesday	wednesday	thursday	friday	saturday
food:	food:	food:	food:	food:	food:	food:
notes:	notes:	notes:	notes:	notes:	notes:	notes:
food:	food:	food:	food:	food:	food:	food:
notes:	notes:	notes:	notes:	notes:	notes:	notes:
food:	food:	food:	food:	food:	food:	food:
notes:	notes:	notes:	notes:	notes:	notes:	notes:
food:	food:	food:	food:	food:	food:	food:
notes:	notes:	notes:	notes:	notes:	notes:	notes:
food:	food:	food:	food:	food:	food:	food:
notes:	notes:	notes:	notes:	notes:	notes:	notes:

single ingredient purees

TYPICALLY 4 TO 6 MONTHS

These single ingredient purees are the building
blocks of all that's to come—the basics. There's nothing
more exciting than feeding your baby his or her
first bites of these wholesome ingredients.

For all the recipes in this chapter, adjust the texture to achieve the desired consistency by adding a little breast milk, formula, or water to thin out the puree.

If you're steaming on the stovetop, when the water is boiling vigorously, turn the heat down to medium-low once the ingredient has been added, then cover and continue steaming as described.

Purees can be refrigerated in airtight containers for 3 days or frozen for up to 2 months. See page 18 for freezing instructions.

Generally, babies this age consume 1 teaspoon to 2 tablespoons per feeding (one feeding per day).

Apple Puree 31

Sweet Potato Puree 32

Carrot Puree 35

Cauliflower Puree 36

Butternut or Acorn Squash Puree 37

Pumpkin Puree 38

Pear Puree 40

Pea Puree 41

Banana Puree 42

Spinach or Kale Puree 43

Mango Puree 44

Broccoli Puree 45

Plum Puree 47

Avocado Puree 48

apple puree

2 small apples, peeled, cored, and cut into ½- to ¾-inch cubes (about 1 cup)

Apple puree (aka applesauce) is one of my all-time favorite things to make in a baby food maker because it is so easy and delicious. Whatever your baby doesn't finish, you can enjoy! Apples are easy on baby's tummy. Whenever Ben is getting over a little sickness, I make apple puree for him. I like using mild apples, like Gala, Red Delicious, Honeycrisp, or Fuji.

water level

COOKING TIME: 25 minutes

Pour water into the tank to the highest level (mine is level 3, which equals about 1 cup water).

Put the apple in the steamer basket or cooking compartment.

Start the cooking process. When the cooking process is done, pour the apple into the blending bowl with the cooking liquid. Blend.

fillable tank

COOKING TIME: 20 minutes

Fill the water tank with water.

Place the apple in the blending bowl.

Set the steam timer for 20 minutes. When the timer goes off, blend the apple with the cooking liquid.

stovetop

COOKING TIME: 13 minutes

In a 2-quart saucepan set over high heat, bring 1 cup water to a boil, about 3 minutes. Add the apple, reduce the heat to medium-low, and place a tight-fitting lid on the saucepan. Steam for about 10 minutes, or until the apple cubes are easily pierced with a fork.

Transfer the apple to a blender (or food processor) with the remaining cooking liquid and blend until smooth.

STORAGE INFORMATION
3 days refrigerator
2 months freezer

sweet potato puree

1 large sweet potato, peeled and cut into ½- to ¾-inch cubes (about 2 cups)

Sweet potato puree is fantastic as baby's first food! Sweet potatoes are a powerhouse of nutrition: high in vitamins A and C, which promote healthy, eyes, skin, and immune system, as well as high in fiber and other beneficial vitamins and minerals. Sweet potatoes take on a gentle sweetness and are easy for baby to digest. And they're a great first food because they combine very well with other foods and spices.

water level
COOKING TIME: 25 minutes

Pour water into the tank to the highest level (mine is level 3, which equals about 1 cup water).

Put the sweet potato in the steamer basket or cooking compartment.

Start the cooking process. When the cooking process is done, pour the sweet potato into the blending bowl with the cooking liquid. Blend.

fillable tank
COOKING TIME: 25 minutes

Fill the water tank with water.

Place the sweet potato in the blending bowl.

Set the steam timer for 25 minutes. When the timer goes off, blend the sweet potato with the cooking liquid.

stovetop
COOKING TIME: 15 minutes

In a 2-quart saucepan set over high heat, bring 1 cup water to a boil, about 3 minutes. Add the sweet potato, reduce the heat to medium-low, and place a tight-fitting lid on the saucepan. Steam for 10 to 12 minutes, until the sweet potato cubes are easily pierced with a fork.

Transfer the sweet potato to a blender (or food processor) with the remaining cooking liquid and blend until smooth.

STORAGE INFORMATION
3 days refrigerator
2 months freezer

carrot puree

3 large carrots, peeled and cut into ½-inch slices (about 2 cups)

This carrot puree has a vibrant orange color. Carrots are full of nutrients like beta-carotene, vitamins A, K, and C, potassium, and fiber, and they are very budget friendly to buy—even organic! My son has loved carrots in every form: pureed, smashed, and in little steamed pieces.

water level
COOKING TIME: 25 minutes

Pour water into the tank to the highest level (mine is level 3, which equals about 1 cup water).

Put the carrot in the steamer basket or cooking compartment.

Start the cooking process. When the cooking process is done, pour the carrot in the blending bowl with the cooking liquid. Blend.

fillable tank
COOKING TIME: 25 minutes

Fill the water tank with water.

Place the carrot in the blending bowl.

Set the steam timer for 25 minutes. When the timer goes off, blend the carrot with the cooking liquid.

stovetop
COOKING TIME: 15 minutes

In a 2-quart saucepan set over high heat, bring the carrots and 1 cup water (or enough water to almost cover the carrot) to a boil, about 3 minutes. Reduce the heat to medium-low and place a tight-fitting lid on the saucepan. Steam for about 12 minutes, or until the carrot slices are easily pierced with a fork.

Transfer the carrot to a blender (or food processor) with the remaining cooking liquid and process until smooth.

NOTE: Be sure to peel the carrots to remove any grit or fibers. When baby is able to have thicker purees or soft carrot pieces, it's okay to leave them unpeeled before cooking.

STORAGE INFORMATION
3 days refrigerator
2 months freezer

cauliflower puree

2 cups (1-inch pieces) cauliflower

Cauliflower blends so smoothly into a velvety puree that your baby will love. Plus, you can use the stems as well as the florets, so nothing goes to waste! Cauliflower is very mild in flavor, so baby will gobble it right up.

water level
COOKING TIME: 25 minutes

Pour water into the tank to the highest level (mine is level 3, which equals about 1 cup water).

Put the cauliflower in the steamer basket or cooking compartment.

Start the cooking process. When the cooking process is done, pour the cauliflower in the blending bowl with the cooking liquid. Blend.

fillable tank
COOKING TIME: 20 minutes

Fill the water tank with water.

Place the cauliflower in the blending bowl.

Set the steam timer for 20 minutes. When the timer goes off, blend the cauliflower with the cooking liquid.

stovetop
COOKING TIME: 13 minutes

In a 2-quart saucepan set over high heat, bring the cauliflower and 1 cup water (or enough water to almost cover the cauliflower) to a boil, about 3 minutes. Reduce the heat to medium-low and place a tight-fitting lid on the saucepan. Steam for about 10 minutes, or until the cauliflower pieces are easily pierced with a fork.

Transfer the cauliflower to a blender (or food processor) with the remaining cooking liquid and process until smooth.

NOTE: It's fine to use the stalks as well as the florets when steaming the cauliflower for puree. As chewing becomes easier for baby, it's okay to give little pieces of softened, steamed stalk or stem parts.

STORAGE INFORMATION
3 days refrigerator
2 months freezer

butternut or acorn squash puree

1½ to 2 cups (½- to ¾-inch cubes) peeled and seeded butternut or acorn squash

Butternut and acorn squashes are not the easiest vegetables to peel and chop, but it's worth it! You really have to put your arm into it. Using a sharp knife, peel the squash and discard the insides and seeds. Squash provides vitamins A and C in abundance, and there's more potassium in 1 cup of butternut or acorn squash than in a banana!

water level

COOKING TIME: 25 minutes

Pour water into the tank to the highest level (mine is level 3, which equals about 1 cup water).

Put the squash in the steamer basket or cooking compartment.

Start the cooking process. When the cooking process is done, pour the squash into the blending bowl with the cooking liquid. Blend.

fillable tank

COOKING TIME: 25 minutes

Fill the water tank with water.

Place the squash in the blending bowl.

Set the steam timer for 25 minutes. When the timer goes off, blend the squash with the cooking liquid.

stovetop

COOKING TIME: 15 minutes

In a 2-quart saucepan set over high heat, bring 1 cup water to a boil, about 3 minutes. Add the squash, reduce the heat to medium-low, and place a tight-fitting lid on the saucepan. Steam for 10 to 12 minutes, until the squash cubes are easily pierced with a fork.

Transfer the squash to a blender (or food processor) with the remaining cooking liquid and blend until smooth.

STORAGE INFORMATION
3 days refrigerator
2 months freezer

pumpkin puree

1½ to 2 cups (½- to ¾-inch cubes) peeled and cleaned pumpkin

Pumpkin, like winter squash, can be a little difficult to prep. I've found the easiest way to tackle cleaning a pumpkin is by cutting it into manageable larger pieces, and then peeling, seeding, and chopping down from there. Pumpkins are available in the fall at farmers' markets and at your grocery store.

water level
COOKING TIME: 25 minutes

Pour water into the tank to the highest level (mine is level 3, which equals about 1 cup water).

Put the pumpkin in the steamer basket or cooking compartment.

Start the cooking process. When the cooking process is done, pour the pumpkin into the blending bowl with the cooking liquid. Blend.

fillable tank
COOKING TIME: 25 minutes

Fill the water tank with water.

Place the pumpkin in the blending bowl.

Set the steam timer for 25 minutes. When the timer goes off, blend the pumpkin with the cooking liquid.

stovetop
COOKING TIME: 15 minutes

In a 2-quart saucepan set over high heat, bring 1 cup water to a boil, about 3 minutes. Add the pumpkin, reduce the heat to medium-low, and place a tight-fitting lid on the saucepan. Steam for 10 to 12 minutes, until the pumpkin cubes are easily pierced with a fork.

Transfer the pumpkin to a blender (or food processor) with the remaining cooking liquid and blend until smooth.

NOTE: You can use this homemade puree in place of canned pumpkin puree in recipes. Looking to make a super easy pumpkin pie with only five ingredients? I've included a recipe and directions at sweetphi.com/extras.

STORAGE INFORMATION
3 days refrigerator
2 months freezer

pear
puree

2 ripe pears, peeled, cored, and cut into slices (about 2 cups)

Pears are a great source of antioxidants, flavonoids, and dietary fiber, as well as many vitamins and minerals. Check for ripeness by gently pressing on the pear's neck; if the skin yields slightly to your touch, it is ripe enough to eat. Want to slow down the ripening process? Put the pear in the fridge. Overly ripe pears have a very mealy texture, so I like to cook pears just a little, making them pliable enough for a puree but not mealy.

water level
COOKING TIME: 10 minutes

Pour water into the tank to the lowest level (mine is level 1, which equals about ⅓ cup water).

Put the pear in the steamer basket or cooking compartment.

Start the cooking process. When the cooking process is done, pour the pear into the blending bowl with the cooking liquid. Blend.

fillable tank
COOKING TIME: 5 minutes

Fill the water tank with water.

Place the pear in the blending bowl.

Set the steam timer for 5 minutes. When the timer goes off, blend the pear with the cooking liquid.

stovetop
COOKING TIME: 4 minutes

In a 2-quart saucepan set over high heat, bring ½ cup water to a boil, about 2 minutes. Add the pear, reduce the heat to medium-low, and place a tight-fitting lid on the saucepan. Steam for about 2 minutes, or until the pear slices are easily pierced with a fork.

Transfer the pear to a blender (or food processor) with the remaining cooking liquid and blend until smooth.

STORAGE INFORMATION
3 days refrigerator
2 months freezer

pea
puree

**1½ cups fresh or
frozen peas**

Peas contain a surprising amount of protein, in addition to other vitamins and minerals, so they're a great first food. They can be purchased fresh or frozen, and I love keeping a bag of organic peas in the freezer so I can make a puree with zero prep—no thawing, peeling, or chopping required. Note that it is quite difficult to get peas silky smooth. If you want them smoother, add a little more liquid and keep blending until the desired consistency is reached.

water level
COOKING TIME: 17 minutes

Pour water into the tank to the middle level (mine is level 2, which equals about ⅔ cup water).

Put the peas in the steamer basket or cooking compartment.

Start the cooking process. When the cooking process is done, pour the peas into the blending bowl with the cooking liquid. Blend.

fillable tank
COOKING TIME: 10 minutes

Fill the water tank with water.

Place the peas in the blending bowl.

Set the steam timer for 10 minutes. When the timer goes off, blend the peas with the cooking liquid.

stovetop
COOKING TIME: 7 minutes

In a 2-quart saucepan set over high heat, bring ½ cup water to a boil, about 2 minutes. Add the peas, reduce the heat to medium-low, and place a tight-fitting lid on the saucepan. Steam for about 5 minutes, or until the peas are tender when pierced with a fork.

Transfer the peas to a blender (or food processor) with the remaining cooking liquid and blend until smooth.

NOTE: This puree is very freezer friendly. While most purees have a maximum life of 2 months in the freezer, pea puree can last up to 6 months.

STORAGE INFORMATION
3 days refrigerator
6 months freezer

banana puree

2 medium bananas, peeled and cut into 1-inch pieces

When I was pregnant, I couldn't stand bananas, but my son absolutely loves them! The mild sweetness and creamy texture of bananas makes them great for pureeing and combining with other foods. I'm happy to report that I, too, like bananas again.

water level
COOKING TIME: 10 minutes

Pour water into the tank to the lowest level (mine is level 1, which equals about ⅓ cup water).

Put the banana in the steamer basket or cooking compartment.

Start the cooking process. When the cooking process is done, pour the banana into the blending bowl with the cooking liquid. Blend.

fillable tank
COOKING TIME: 5 minutes

Fill the water tank with water.

Place the banana in the blending bowl.

Set the steam timer for 5 minutes. When the timer goes off, blend the banana with the cooking liquid.

stovetop
COOKING TIME: 4 minutes

In a 2-quart saucepan set over high heat, bring ½ cup water to a boil, about 2 minutes. Add the banana, reduce the heat to medium-low, and place a tight-fitting lid on the saucepan. Steam for 2 minutes.

Transfer the banana to a blender (or food processor) with the remaining cooking liquid and blend until smooth.

STORAGE INFORMATION
2 days refrigerator
2 months freezer

spinach or kale puree

2 cups stemmed and coarsely chopped fresh spinach or kale

I use spinach and kale interchangeably. They're both excellent leafy greens that provide water-soluble vitamins and a wide variety of phytonutrients. When raw, spinach or kale can sometimes have a slightly bitter taste, but that disappears after steaming.

water level

COOKING TIME: 17 minutes

Pour water into the tank to the middle level (mine is level 2, which equals about ⅔ cup water).

Put the spinach in the steamer basket or cooking compartment.

Start the cooking process. When the cooking process is done, pour the spinach into the blending bowl with the cooking liquid. Blend.

fillable tank

COOKING TIME: 10 minutes

Fill the water tank with water.

Place the spinach in the blending bowl.

Set the steam timer for 10 minutes. When the timer goes off, blend the spinach with the cooking liquid.

stovetop

COOKING TIME: 4 minutes

In a 2-quart saucepan set over high heat, bring ½ cup water to a boil, about 2 minutes. Add the spinach, reduce the heat to medium-low, and place a tight-fitting lid on the saucepan. Steam for 2 minutes.

Transfer the spinach to a blender (or food processor) with the remaining cooking liquid and blend until smooth.

STORAGE INFORMATION
3 days refrigerator
2 months freezer

mango
puree

2 mangoes, peeled, pitted, and cut into slices, or 1½ cups fresh or frozen mango pieces

When I first gave my son mango puree, he loved it! This tropical fruit contains lots of vitamin C to help boost baby's immune system. Mangoes are definitely a feel-good fruit—they are beautiful to look at, taste great, and blend perfectly for purees—but they can be a little difficult to find fresh when they're not in season. That's when I use frozen organic mango chunks.

water level

COOKING TIME: 10 minutes

Pour water into the tank to the lowest level (mine is level 1, which equals about ⅓ cup water).

Put the mango in the steamer basket or cooking compartment.

Start the cooking process. When the cooking process is done, pour the mango into the blending bowl with the cooking liquid. Blend.

fillable tank

COOKING TIME: 5 minutes

Fill the water tank with water.

Place the mango in the blending bowl.

Set the steam timer for 5 minutes. When the timer goes off, blend the mango with the cooking liquid.

stovetop

COOKING TIME: 4 minutes

In a 2-quart saucepan set over high heat, bring ½ cup water to a boil, about 2 minutes. Add the mango, reduce the heat to medium-low, and place a tight-fitting lid on the saucepan. Steam for about 2 minutes, or until the mango pieces are easily pierced with a fork.

Transfer the mango to a blender (or food processor) with the remaining cooking liquid and blend until smooth.

STORAGE INFORMATION
3 days refrigerator
2 months freezer

broccoli puree

2 cups (1-inch pieces) broccoli (stalk pieces okay; see Note)

I never steam my broccoli (usually roasting or sautéing it instead), so I was amazed that my son loved this version, and I had to try it myself. I was so pleasantly surprised to find that the sometimes bitter taste of broccoli was gone; when steamed, it takes on a slightly sweet flavor. Broccoli is known for its abundance of vitamins C and K, and its high folate and fiber content. We all know we should eat more broccoli, so set the groundwork with this broccoli puree. Also, you can cut up and steam the broccoli stem as well as the florets, so nothing goes to waste.

water level

COOKING TIME: 25 minutes

Pour water into the tank to the highest level (mine is level 3, which equals about 1 cup water).

Put the broccoli in the steamer basket or cooking compartment.

Start the cooking process. When the cooking process is done, pour the broccoli into the blending bowl with the cooking liquid. Blend.

fillable tank

COOKING TIME: 20 minutes

Fill the water tank with water.

Place the broccoli in the blending bowl.

Set the steam timer for 20 minutes. When the timer goes off, blend the broccoli with the cooking liquid.

stovetop

COOKING TIME: 13 minutes

In a 2-quart saucepan set over high heat, bring the broccoli and 1 cup water (or enough to almost cover the broccoli) to a boil, about 3 minutes. Reduce the heat to medium-low and place a tight-fitting lid on the saucepan. Steam for about 10 minutes, or until the broccoli pieces are easily pierced with a fork.

Transfer the broccoli to a blender (or food processor) with the remaining cooking liquid and blend until smooth.

NOTE: If you're using the stalk, peel it just a little so there are no tough pieces. Some babies can get a little gassy when eating broccoli, which is completely normal.

STORAGE INFORMATION
3 days refrigerator
2 months freezer

plum
puree

**3 plums, pitted and sliced
(about 1½ cups)**

Very vibrant in color, this juicy fruit not only is delicious but also helps provide relief from indigestion. If baby is ever stopped up, my first recommendation would be plum puree (it's worked every time for me). I pit the plums when making this puree but leave the skins on.

water level
COOKING TIME: 17 minutes

Pour water into the tank to the middle level (mine is level 2, which equals ⅔ cup water).

Put the plum in the steamer basket or cooking compartment.

Start the cooking process. When the cooking process is done, pour the plum into the blending bowl with the cooking liquid. Blend.

fillable tank
COOKING TIME: 10 minutes

Fill the water tank with water.

Place the plum in the blending bowl.

Set the steam timer for 10 minutes. When the timer goes off, blend the plum with the cooking liquid.

stovetop
COOKING TIME: 8 minutes

In a 2-quart saucepan set over high heat, bring ½ cup water to a boil. about 3 minutes. Add the plums, reduce the heat to medium-low, and place a tight-fitting lid on the saucepan. Steam for about 5 minutes, or until the plum slices are easily pierced with a fork.

Transfer the plum to a blender (or food processor) with the remaining cooking liquid and blend until smooth.

STORAGE INFORMATION
3 days refrigerator
2 months freezer

avocado puree

1 Hass avocado, pit and peel removed, cut into 8 pieces

Avocados are a superfood baby will love. They have a very mild flavor and are high in vitamin K and folate, among other nutrients. You could make avocado puree with very ripe avocados and no steaming, but I find the perfect consistency of avocado puree comes from using avocados that are not overly ripe and then steamed for a few minutes.

water level
COOKING TIME: 10 minutes

Pour water into the tank to the lowest level (mine is level 1, which equals about ⅓ cup water).

Put the avocado in the steamer basket or cooking compartment.

Start the cooking process. When the cooking process is done, pour the avocado into the blending bowl with the cooking liquid. Blend.

fillable tank
COOKING TIME: 5 minutes

Fill the water tank with water.

Place the avocado in the blending bowl.

Set the steam timer for 5 minutes. When the timer goes off, blend the avocado with the cooking liquid.

stovetop
COOKING TIME: 4 minutes

In a 2-quart saucepan set over high heat, bring ½ cup water to a boil, about 2 minutes. Add the avocado, reduce the heat to medium-low, and place a tight-fitting lid on the saucepan. Steam for 2 minutes.

Transfer the avocado to a blender (or food processor) with the remaining cooking liquid and blend until smooth.

NOTE: This puree is not freezer friendly. It turns brown and has an odd texture when thawed. If baby is just starting to try food, I'd recommend making a half batch.

STORAGE INFORMATION
2 days refrigerator
do not freeze

combination purees

TYPICALLY 6 TO 7 MONTHS

Once you've gone through the basics—the single
ingredient purees—then you can add new fruits
and vegetables to the one's baby has already tried,
like building with blocks.

If baby has already had apple, that's a good base—or
building block—for trying other things, like beets! These
purees can be made smooth or left a little chunkier
so baby can start learning about new textures. If the
puree is too thick, add a little bit of liquid (breast milk,
formula, or water) to reach the desired consistency.

Apple, Beet, and Cherry Puree 53

Apple and Beet Puree 55

Apple, Beet, and Strawberry Puree 56

Apple, Broccoli, and Pea Puree 57

Apple, Broccoli, and Kale Puree 58

Apple, Corn, and Sweet Potato Puree 60

Apple, Kiwi, and Spinach Puree 61

Apricot, Winter Squash, and Banana Puree 62

Avocado and Cherry Puree 63

Asparagus, Avocado, and Mango Puree 65

Parsnip, Beet, and Sweet Potato Puree 66

Bell Pepper and Sweet Potato Puree 67

Berry and Sweet Potato Puree 68

Berry and Squash Puree 71

Blueberry, Melon, and Pear Puree 72

Broccoli, Mango, and Zucchini Puree 74

Carrot, Peach, and Pumpkin Puree 75

Carrot, Pear, and Sweet Potato Puree 77

Cauliflower, Plum, and Date Puree 78

Corn, Pear, and Cauliflower Puree 79

Green Bean, Kale, and Pea Puree 80

Green Bean and Squash Puree 82

Mango, Pineapple, and Pumpkin Puree 83

Nectarine, Peach, and Sweet Potato Puree 84

Winter and Summer Squash Puree 85

Baby "Cereals" and Grains 86

Introducing Meat, Poultry, and Fish Purees 87

apple, beet, and cherry puree

1 medium apple, peeled, cored, and cut into ½- to ¾-inch cubes (about 1 cup)

1 medium beet, peeled and cut into ½- to ¾-inch cubes

1 cup cherries, pitted

Apples, beets, and cherries make a sweet and slightly tart puree. This vibrant mixture can stain bibs, so use either a dark-colored one or a bib you're not fond of. Cherries are grown in my home state of Wisconsin, so I love making this puree when they are in season. But I also secretly love buying the pitted cherries from the freezer section, because the work of pitting cherries has been done for me already!

water level
COOKING TIME: 25 minutes

Pour water into the tank to the highest level (mine is level 3, which equals about 1 cup of water).

Put the apple, beet, and cherries in the steamer basket or cooking compartment.

Start the cooking process. When the cooking process is done, pour the apple, beet, and cherries into the blending bowl with the cooking liquid. Blend.

fillable tank
COOKING TIME: 20 minutes

Fill the water tank with water.

Place the apple, beet, and cherries in the blending bowl.

Set the steam timer for 20 minutes. When the timer goes off, blend the apple, beet, and cherries with the cooking liquid.

stovetop
COOKING TIME: 13 minutes

In a 2-quart saucepan over high heat, bring 1 cup water to a boil, about 3 minutes. Add the apple, beet, and cherries; reduce the heat to medium-low; and place a tight-fitting lid on the saucepan. Steam for about 10 minutes, or until the apple and beet cubes are easily pierced with a fork.

Transfer the apple, beet, and cherries to a blender (or food processor) with the remaining cooking liquid and blend until smooth.

STORAGE INFORMATION
3 days refrigerator
2 months freezer

apple
and
beet puree

1 medium apple, peeled, cored, and cut into ½- to ¾-inch cubes (about 1 cup)

2 medium beets, peeled and cut into ½- to ¾-inch cubes

Babies love beets! That's surprising to me, because beets are such a polarizing food for adults. Among mothers I've spoken with, we all agree: we were so amazed by how much our babies loved beets. Mix them with apples (or cherries or strawberries—all recipes on the following pages) for vibrantly colored purees baby will love.

water level
COOKING TIME: 25 minutes

Pour water into the tank to the highest level (mine is level 3, which equals about 1 cup of water).

Put the apple and beet in the steamer basket or cooking compartment.

Start the cooking process. When the cooking process is done, pour the apple and beet into the blending bowl with the cooking liquid. Blend.

fillable tank
COOKING TIME: 20 minutes

Fill the water tank with water.

Place the apple and beet in the blending bowl.

Set the steam timer for 20 minutes. When the timer goes off, blend the apple and beet with the cooking liquid.

stovetop
COOKING TIME: 13 minutes

In a 2-quart saucepan set over high heat, bring 1 cup water to a boil, about 3 minutes. Add the apple and beet, reduce the heat to medium-low, and place a tight-fitting lid on the saucepan. Steam for about 10 minutes, or until the apple and beet cubes are easily pierced with a fork.

Transfer the apple and beet to a blender (or food processor) with the remaining cooking liquid and blend until smooth.

NOTE: There are many varieties of beets, not just the bright red ones! Try golden beets, candy-striped beets, or white beets, especially if you don't want to deal with the bright-red stains that red beets leave behind.

STORAGE INFORMATION
3 days refrigerator
2 months freezer

apple, beet, and strawberry puree

1 medium apple, peeled, cored, and cut into ½- to ¾-inch cubes (about 1 cup)

1 medium beet, peeled and cut into ½- to ¾-inch cubes

1 cup strawberries, hulled

Beets have a slightly sweet and earthy flavor by themselves, so when combined with apple and strawberries, the end result is a puree babies will enjoy. For this recipe, I like using a candy stripe or yellow beet as they're even sweeter than red beets.

water level
COOKING TIME: 25 minutes

Pour water into the tank to the highest level (mine is level 3, which equals about 1 cup of water).

Put the apple, beet, and strawberries in the steamer basket or cooking compartment.

Start the cooking process. When the cooking process is done, pour the apple, beet, and strawberries into the blending bowl with the cooking liquid. Blend.

fillable tank
COOKING TIME: 20 minutes

Fill the water tank with water.

Place the apple, beet, and strawberries in the blending bowl.

Set the steam timer for 20 minutes. When the timer goes off, blend the apple, beet, and strawberries with the cooking liquid.

stovetop
COOKING TIME: 13 minutes

In a 2-quart saucepan over high heat, bring 1 cup water to a boil, about 3 minutes. Add the apple, beet, and strawberries; reduce the heat to medium-low; and place a tight-fitting lid on the saucepan. Steam for about 10 minutes, or until the apple and beet cubes are easily pierced with a fork.

Transfer the apple, beet, and strawberries to a blender (or food processor) with the remaining cooking liquid and process until smooth.

STORAGE INFORMATION
3 days refrigerator
2 months freezer

apple, broccoli, and pea puree

1 medium apple, peeled, cored, and cut into ½- to ¾-inch cubes (about 1 cup)

1 cup (1-inch pieces) broccoli (stalk pieces okay)

½ cup fresh or frozen peas

The vibrant color and mild flavor of this puree will have babies opening their mouths for bite after bite. This puree can be made super smooth by a little extra liquid, or you can leave it a little thicker so your baby can experience different textures. Although you can buy fresh spring peas, they are sometimes difficult to find, so I often just buy a bag of frozen organic peas.

water level

COOKING TIME: 25 minutes

Pour water into the tank to the highest level (mine is level 3, which equals about 1 cup water).

Put the apple, broccoli, and peas in the steamer basket or cooking compartment.

Start the cooking process. When the cooking process is done, pour the apple, broccoli, and peas into the blending bowl with the cooking liquid. Blend.

fillable tank

COOKING TIME: 20 minutes

Fill the water tank with water.

Place the apple, broccoli, and peas in the blending bowl.

Set the steam timer for 20 minutes. When the timer goes off, blend the apple, broccoli, and peas with the cooking liquid.

stovetop

COOKING TIME: 13 minutes

In a 2-quart saucepan set over high heat, bring 1 cup water to a boil, about 3 minutes. Add the apple, broccoli, and peas; reduce the heat to medium-low; and place a tight-fitting lid on the saucepan. Steam for about 10 minutes, or until the apple and broccoli pieces are easily pierced with a fork.

Transfer the apple, broccoli, and peas to a blender (or food processor) with the remaining cooking liquid and blend until smooth.

STORAGE INFORMATION
3 days refrigerator
2 months freezer

apple, broccoli, and kale puree

1 medium apple, peeled, cored, and cut into ½- to ¾-inch cubes (about 1 cup)

1 cup (1-inch pieces) broccoli (stalk pieces okay)

½ cup stemmed and coarsely chopped kale or spinach

I never would have thought to combine apple with broccoli, but one day I made individual-ingredient apple and broccoli purees. I must have been low on sleep, because I combined them once they were prepped. I fed some to my son to see if he'd like it—and I'd never seen him eat so much! In this puree, I add a little bit of kale (or spinach; I use them interchangeably based on what I have on hand) for a bright green treat baby will love.

water level
COOKING TIME: 25 minutes

Pour water into the tank to the highest level (mine is level 3, which equals about 1 cup of water).

Put the apple, broccoli, and kale in the steamer basket or cooking compartment.

Start the cooking process. When the cooking process is done, pour the apple, broccoli, and kale in the blending bowl with the cooking liquid. Blend.

fillable tank
COOKING TIME: 20 minutes

Fill the water tank with water.

Place the apple, broccoli, and kale in the blending bowl.

Set the steam timer for 20 minutes. When the timer goes off, blend the apple, broccoli, and kale with the cooking liquid.

stovetop
COOKING TIME: 13 minutes

In a 2-quart saucepan set over high heat, bring 1 cup water to a boil, about 3 minutes. Add the apple, broccoli, and kale; reduce the heat to medium-low; and place a tight-fitting lid on the saucepan. Steam for about 10 minutes, or until the apple and broccoli pieces are easily pierced with a fork.

Transfer the apple, broccoli, and kale to a blender (or food processor) with the remaining cooking liquid and blend until smooth.

STORAGE INFORMATION
3 days refrigerator
2 months freezer

apple, corn, and sweet potato puree

1 medium apple, peeled, cored, and cut into ½- to ¾-inch cubes (about 1 cup)

½ cup corn kernels, frozen or freshly cut from 1 ear

1 medium sweet potato, peeled and cut into small cubes (about 1 cup)

This gentle orange puree has a delicious, mild sweetness baby will love (and you, the taste tester, will love too). Before I started making baby food at home, one of the jars of food I came across was apple, corn, and sweet potato. My son loved it. So when I started making purees, I re-created that flavor combination at home, and he continues to love it!

water level
COOKING TIME: 25 minutes

Pour water into the tank to the highest level (mine is level 3, which equals about 1 cup water).

Put the apple, corn, and sweet potato in the steamer basket or cooking compartment.

Start the cooking process. When the cooking process is done, pour the apple, corn, and sweet potato into the blending bowl with the cooking liquid. Blend.

fillable tank
COOKING TIME: 20 minutes

Fill the water tank with water.

Place the apple, corn, and sweet potato into the blending bowl.

Set the steam timer for 20 minutes. When the timer goes off, blend the apple, corn, and sweet potato with the cooking liquid.

stovetop
COOKING TIME: 13 minutes

In a 2-quart saucepan set over high heat, bring 1 cup water to a boil, about 3 minutes. Add the apple, corn, and sweet potato; reduce the heat to medium-low; and place a tight-fitting lid on the saucepan. Steam for about 10 minutes, or until the apple and sweet potato cubes are easily pierced with a fork.

Transfer the apple, corn, and sweet potato to a blender (or food processor) with the remaining cooking liquid and blend until smooth.

STORAGE INFORMATION
3 days refrigerator
2 months freezer

apple, kiwi, and spinach puree

1 medium apple, peeled, cored, and cut into ½- to ¾-inch cubes (about 1 cup)

1 cup stemmed and torn spinach or kale leaves

2 kiwifruits, peel removed and cut into a few large pieces

Sweet and tangy, the kiwifruit gives this bright green puree an ample dose of wonderful vitamins C, K, and E, as well as folate and potassium. Although edible, I suggest removing the fuzzy brown peel of the kiwi when making this puree (see Note), as leaving it on will add a gritty texture. When baby starts eating solids, try serving them a few pieces of soft kiwi while the rest is cooking.

water level
COOKING TIME: 25 minutes

Pour water into the tank to the highest level (mine is level 3, which equals about 1 cup water).

Put the apple, spinach, and kiwi in the steamer basket or cooking compartment.

Start the cooking process. When the cooking process is done, pour the apple, spinach, and kiwi in the blending bowl with the cooking liquid. Blend.

fillable tank
COOKING TIME: 20 minutes

Fill the water tank with water.

Place the apple, spinach, and kiwi into the blending bowl.

Set the steam timer for 20 minutes. When the timer goes off, blend the apple, spinach, and kiwi with the cooking liquid.

stovetop
COOKING TIME: 13 minutes

In a 2-quart saucepan set over high heat, bring 1 cup water to a boil, about 3 minutes. Add the apple, spinach, and kiwi; reduce the heat to medium-low; and place a tight-fitting lid on the saucepan. Steam for about 10 minutes, or until the apple cubes are easily pierced with a fork.

Transfer the apple, spinach, and kiwi to a blender (or food processor) with the remaining cooking liquid and blend until smooth.

NOTE: To remove the peel from the kiwi, cut the kiwi in half and then scoop out the insides using a spoon.

STORAGE INFORMATION
3 days refrigerator
2 months freezer

apricot, winter squash, and banana puree

2 apricots, halved and pitted

1 cup (½- to ¾-inch cubes) peeled and seeded butternut squash

½ medium banana, peeled and sliced

The beautiful warm color of this puree is surpassed only by its amazing taste! Apricots are a great source of vitamin A, which supports baby's developing eye health. If the squash is too difficult to find (or hard to peel), you can always substitute peeled sweet potato. I like adding the banana after the squash and apricots have cooked, letting it get warm and a little soft for a minute from the residual heat before blending the puree.

water level

COOKING TIME: 25 minutes

Pour water into the tank to the highest level (mine is level 3, which equals 1 cup water).

Put the apricot and squash in the steamer basket or cooking compartment.

Start the cooking process. When the cooking process is done, pour the apricot and squash into the blending bowl with the cooking liquid. Add the banana. Wait 1 minute, then blend.

fillable tank

COOKING TIME: 25 minutes

Fill the water tank with water.

Place the apricot and squash in the blending bowl.

Set the steam timer for 25 minutes. When the timer goes off, add the banana. Wait 1 minute, then blend with the cooking liquid.

stovetop

COOKING TIME: 14 minutes

In a 2-quart saucepan set over high heat, bring 1 cup water to a boil, about 3 minutes. Add the squash, reduce the heat to medium-low, and place a tight-fitting lid on the saucepan. Steam for 8 minutes, then add the apricot and steam for another 2 to 3 minutes, until the squash cubes are easily pierced with a fork. Add the banana, remove from the heat, take off the lid, and wait 1 minute.

Transfer the squash, apricot, and banana to a blender (or food processor) with the remaining cooking liquid and blend until smooth.

STORAGE INFORMATION
3 days refrigerator
2 months freezer

avocado and cherry puree

1 Hass avocado, pit and peel removed, quartered

1 cup dark cherries, pitted

This puree is a powerful superfood combination for baby. Avocado's nutritional benefits are innumerable, and cherries bring some mighty benefits to the high chair as well. Cherries contain natural melatonin, which helps regulate the body's internal clock, so if your baby is a little off his or her sleep schedule, this puree might just do the trick. There are sweet (dark) and sour cherry varieties, and both are okay to use.

water level

COOKING TIME: 10 minutes

Pour water into the tank to the lowest level (mine is level 1, which equals about ⅓ cup water).

Put the avocado and cherries in the steamer basket or cooking compartment.

Start the cooking process. When the cooking process is done, pour the avocado and cherries into the blending bowl with the cooking liquid. Blend.

fillable tank

COOKING TIME: 5 minutes

Fill the water tank with water.

Place the avocado and cherries into the blending bowl.

Set the steam timer for 5 minutes. When the timer goes off, blend the avocado and cherries with the cooking liquid.

stovetop

COOKING TIME: 4 minutes

In a 2-quart saucepan set over high heat, bring ½ cup water to a boil, about 2 minutes. Add the avocado and cherries, reduce the heat to medium-low, and place a tight-fitting lid on the saucepan. Steam for 2 minutes.

Transfer the avocado and cherries to a blender (or food processor) with the remaining cooking liquid and blend until smooth.

NOTE: This puree is not freezer friendly, as it turns a dark brown color and has an odd texture when thawed. If baby is just starting to try food, I'd recommend making a half batch.

STORAGE INFORMATION
3 days refrigerator
do not freeze

asparagus, avocado, and mango puree

2 asparagus stalks, tough ends removed

½ Hass avocado, pit and peel removed, quartered

½ cup chopped fresh or frozen mango

This puree reminds me of a fancy spring salad. Bright, fresh asparagus is mixed with creamy avocado and mango, resulting in silky smooth goodness! Asparagus is a great source of iron, calcium, and vitamin A, among other nutrients, and is best when it's in season during the spring. Asparagus can give some babies gas, so mixing it with avocado, which can settle the stomach, provides the perfect balance of greens.

water level
COOKING TIME: 17 minutes

Pour water into the tank to the medium level (mine is level 2, which equals about ⅔ cup water).

Put the asparagus, avocado, and mango in the steamer basket or cooking compartment.

Start the cooking process. When the cooking process is done, pour the asparagus, avocado, and mango into the blending bowl with the cooking liquid. Blend.

fillable tank
COOKING TIME: 10 minutes

Fill the water tank with water.

Place the asparagus, avocado, and mango into the blending bowl.

Set the steam timer for 10 minutes. When the timer goes off, blend the asparagus, avocado, and mango with the cooking liquid.

stovetop
COOKING TIME: 7 minutes

In a 2-quart saucepan set over high heat, bring ½ cup water to a boil, about 2 minutes. Add the asparagus, avocado, and mango; reduce the heat to medium-low; and place a tight-fitting lid on the saucepan. Steam for about 5 minutes, or until the asparagus stalks are tender when pierced with a fork.

Transfer the asparagus, avocado, and mango to a blender (or food processor) with the remaining cooking liquid and blend until smooth.

STORAGE INFORMATION
3 days refrigerator
2 months freezer

parsnip, beet, and sweet potato puree

1 large parsnip, peeled and cut into ½-inch slices (about ¾ cup)

1 medium beet, peeled and cut into ¾-inch cubes (about ½ cup)

1 medium sweet potato, peeled and cut into ½- to ¾-inch cubes (about 1 cup)

Parsnips are root vegetables closely related to the carrot. In fact, it looks like a white carrot and can be found next to the carrots in most grocery stores. I am very proud that I've introduced many people to the vegetable by adding a parsnip when I make mashed potatoes sometimes. Here, I combine parsnip with other root vegetables (beet and sweet potato) to make a hearty puree for baby.

water level
COOKING TIME: 25 minutes

Pour water into the tank to the highest level (mine is level 3, which equals about 1 cup water).

Put the parsnip, beet, and sweet potato in the steamer basket or cooking compartment.

Start the cooking process. When the cooking process is done, pour the parsnip, beet, and sweet potato into the blending bowl with the cooking liquid. Blend.

fillable tank
COOKING TIME: 25 minutes

Fill the water tank with water.

Place the parsnip, beet, and sweet potato in the blending bowl.

Set the steam timer for 25 minutes. When the timer goes off, blend the parsnip, beet, and sweet potato with the cooking liquid.

stovetop
COOKING TIME: 13 minutes

In a 2-quart saucepan set over high heat, bring 1 cup water to a boil, about 3 minutes. Add the parsnip, beet, and sweet potato; reduce the heat to medium-low; and place a tight-fitting lid on the saucepan. Steam for about 10 minutes, or until the vegetables are easily pierced with a fork.

Transfer the parsnip, beet, and sweet potato to a blender (or food processor) with the remaining cooking liquid and blend until smooth.

NOTE: There are many varieties of beets, not just the bright red ones! Try golden beets, candy-striped beets, or white beets if you don't want to deal with the bright-red stains that red beets leave behind.

STORAGE INFORMATION
3 days refrigerator
2 months freezer

bell pepper and sweet potato puree

1 medium sweet potato, peeled and cut into ½- to ¾-inch cubes (about 1 cup)

1 medium bell pepper, seeds and ribs removed, cut into strips (about 1 cup)

Bell pepper is not commonly found in purees, but it should be! Combined with sweet potato, it has an almost sweet taste. While there are different varieties of bell peppers, I like to use the red, yellow, or orange ones for the vitamin C. Bell peppers are also a fantastic source of vitamin A (from beta-carotene), vitamin B_6, folate, and potassium.

water level
COOKING TIME: 25 minutes

Pour water into the tank to the highest level (mine is level 3, which equals about 1 cup water).

Put the sweet potato and bell pepper in the steamer basket or cooking compartment.

Start the cooking process. When the cooking process is done, pour the sweet potato and bell pepper into the blending bowl with the cooking liquid. Blend.

fillable tank
COOKING TIME: 25 minutes

Fill the water tank with water.

Place the sweet potato and bell pepper in the blending bowl.

Set the steam timer for 25 minutes. When the timer goes off, blend the sweet potato and bell pepper with the cooking liquid.

stovetop
COOKING TIME: 13 minutes

In a 2-quart saucepan set over high heat, bring 1 cup water to a boil, about 3 minutes. Add the sweet potato and bell pepper, reduce the heat to medium-low, and place a tight-fitting lid on the saucepan. Steam for about 10 minutes, or until the sweet potato cubes are easily pierced with a fork.

Transfer the sweet potato and bell pepper to a blender (or food processor) with the remaining cooking liquid and blend until smooth.

NOTES: If the puree is too thick, add a little bit of liquid (breast milk, formula, or water) to reach the desired consistency.

Red, yellow, and orange bell peppers tend to be slightly sweeter than the green ones, but all colors are fine to use here.

STORAGE INFORMATION
3 days refrigerator
2 months freezer

berry and sweet potato puree

1 medium sweet potato, peeled and cut into ½- to ¾-inch cubes (about 1 cup)

1 cup fresh or frozen raspberries or other berries

A puree made of berries alone can be a little watery and seedy. However, when mixed with sweet potatoes, the resulting puree is silky smooth in texture and a beautiful reddish-orange color. I like using raspberries (known as nature's candy) in this puree because of their sweetness, but any berry—or a mix—would work.

water level
COOKING TIME: 25 minutes

Pour water into the tank to the highest level (mine is level 3, which equals about 1 cup water).

Put the sweet potato and raspberries in the steamer basket or cooking compartment.

Start the cooking process. When the cooking process is done, pour the sweet potato and raspberries into the blending bowl with the cooking liquid. Blend.

fillable tank
COOKING TIME: 25 minutes

Fill the water tank with water.

Place the sweet potato and raspberries into the blending bowl.

Set the steam timer for 25 minutes. When the timer goes off, blend the sweet potato and raspberries with the cooking liquid.

stovetop
COOKING TIME: 13 minutes

In a 2-quart saucepan set over high heat, bring 1 cup water to a boil, about 3 minutes. Add the sweet potato and raspberries, reduce the heat to medium-low, and place a tight-fitting lid on the saucepan. Steam for about 10 minutes, or until the sweet potato cubes are easily pierced with a fork.

Transfer the sweet potato and raspberries to a blender (or food processor) with the remaining cooking liquid and blend until smooth.

STORAGE INFORMATION
3 days refrigerator
2 months freezer

berry and squash puree

1 cup (½- to 1-inch) cubed squash

1 cup fresh or frozen berries

In this puree, you could use summer squash (zucchini) or winter squash (butternut squash) and any combination of berries you'd like. In the summertime, I like making this with zucchini and blueberries. Nutrients are found in the skin of zucchini, so don't worry about peeling it, but if you're using winter squash, be sure to remove the hard skin.

water level

COOKING TIME:
SUMMER SQUASH 17 minutes
WINTER SQUASH 25 minutes

If you're using summer squash, pour water into the tank to the medium level (mine is level 2, which equals about ⅔ cup water).

If you're using winter squash, pour water into the tank to the highest level (mine is level 3, which equals about 1 cup water).

Put the squash and berries in the steamer basket or cooking compartment.

Start the cooking process. When the cooking process is done, pour the squash and berries into the blending bowl with the cooking liquid. Blend.

fillable tank

COOKING TIME:
SUMMER SQUASH 15 minutes
WINTER SQUASH 25 minutes

Fill the water tank with water.

Place the squash and berries into the blending bowl.

If you're using summer squash, set the steam timer for 15 minutes.

If you're using winter squash, set the steam timer for 25 minutes.

When the timer goes off, blend the squash and berries with the cooking liquid.

stovetop

COOKING TIME:
SUMMER SQUASH 8 minutes
WINTER SQUASH 13 minutes

In a 2-quart saucepan set over high heat, bring 1 cup water to a boil, about 3 minutes. Add the squash and berries, reduce the heat to medium-low, and place a tight-fitting lid on the saucepan.

If you're using summer squash, steam for about 5 minutes, or until easily pierced with a fork.

If you're using winter squash, steam for about 10 minutes, or until easily pierced.

Transfer the squash and berries to a blender (or food processor) with the remaining cooking liquid and blend until smooth.

STORAGE INFORMATION
3 days refrigerator
2 months freezer

blueberry, melon, and pear puree

1 cup blueberries

1 cup cubed cantaloupe, skin and seeds removed

1 medium pear, peeled, cored, and cut into slices (½ to ¾ cup)

This silky smooth puree is super quick to make because the ingredients only need a touch of steam to get them to optimal softness for blending. I like using cantaloupe because of its high beta-carotene, vitamin C, and folate content, but you could use watermelon or honeydew and any type of berries you'd like.

water level

COOKING TIME: 10 minutes

Pour water into the tank to the lowest level (mine is level 1, which equals about ⅓ cup water).

Put the blueberries, cantaloupe, and pear in the steamer basket or cooking compartment.

Start the cooking process. When the cooking process is done, pour the blueberries, cantaloupe, and pear into the blending bowl with the cooking liquid. Blend.

fillable tank

COOKING TIME: 5 minutes

Fill the water tank with water.

Place the blueberries, cantaloupe, and pear into the blending bowl.

Set the steam timer for 5 minutes. When the timer goes off, blend the blueberries, cantaloupe, and pear with the cooking liquid.

stovetop

COOKING TIME: 4 minutes

In a 2-quart saucepan set over high heat, bring ½ cup water to a boil, about 2 minutes. Add the blueberries, cantaloupe, and pear; reduce the heat to medium-low; and place a tight-fitting lid on the saucepan. Steam for about 2 minutes, or until the pear slices are easily pierced with a fork.

Transfer the blueberries, cantaloupe, and pear to a blender (or food processor) with the remaining cooking liquid and blend until smooth.

STORAGE INFORMATION
3 days refrigerator
2 months freezer

broccoli, mango, and zucchini puree

1 cup (1-inch pieces) broccoli (stalk pieces are okay)

1 mango, peeled, pitted, and sliced, or about ¾ cup frozen mango pieces

½ cup diced zucchini (skin on is okay)

As I mentioned in the Apple, Broccoli, and Kale Puree (page 58), I would never have thought to mix broccoli with sweeter ingredients, but my son loves the combination. This super green puree is an excellent source of vitamin C. Because of the high water content of zucchini, this puree has the perfect light and not-too-thick texture.

water level
COOKING TIME: 25 minutes

Pour water into the tank to the highest level (mine is level 3, which equals about 1 cup water).

Put the broccoli, mango, and zucchini in the steamer basket or cooking compartment.

Start the cooking process. When the cooking process is done, pour the broccoli, mango, and zucchini into the blending bowl with the cooking liquid. Blend.

fillable tank
COOKING TIME: 20 minutes

Fill the water tank with water.

Place the broccoli, mango, and zucchini in the blending bowl.

Set the steam timer for 20 minutes. When the timer goes off, blend the broccoli, mango, and zucchini with the cooking liquid.

stovetop
COOKING TIME: 13 minutes

In a 2-quart saucepan set over high heat, bring 1 cup water to a boil, about 3 minutes. Add the broccoli, mango, and zucchini; reduce the heat to medium-low; and place a tight-fitting lid on the saucepan. Steam for about 10 minutes, or until the broccoli pieces are easily pierced with a fork.

Transfer the broccoli, mango, and zucchini to a blender (or food processor) with the remaining cooking liquid and blend until smooth.

STORAGE INFORMATION
3 days refrigerator
2 months freezer

carrot, peach, and pumpkin puree

1 large carrot, peeled and cut into slices (about ½ cup)

1 cup peach slices (from about 2 small peaches)

½ cup (½- to ¾-inch cubes) peeled and cleaned pumpkin

This is the perfect late summer to early fall puree for baby. Peaches are just ending their summertime bounty, and carrots and pumpkins are coming into season. Carrots, peaches, and pumpkin combine to make this slightly sweet, super orange puree, which is high in vitamin A (which helps with eyesight development and promotes healthy skin). If you don't have fresh pumpkin, feel free to substitute with winter squash or sweet potato. You can also use ½ cup canned pumpkin, but the flavor is better with a fresh ingredient.

water level
COOKING TIME: 25 minutes

Pour water into the tank to the highest level (mine is level 3, which equals about 1 cup water).

Put the carrot, peach, and pumpkin in the steamer basket or cooking compartment.

Start the cooking process. When the cooking process is done, pour the carrot, peach, and pumpkin into the blending bowl with the cooking liquid. Blend.

fillable tank
COOKING TIME: 25 minutes

Fill the water tank with water.

Place the carrot, peach, and pumpkin in the blending bowl.

Set the steam timer for 25 minutes. When the timer goes off, blend the carrot, peach, and pumpkin with the cooking liquid.

stovetop
COOKING TIME: 13 minutes

In a 2-quart saucepan set over high heat, bring 1 cup water to a boil, about 3 minutes. Add the carrot, peach, and pumpkin; reduce the heat to medium-low; and place a tight-fitting lid on the saucepan. Steam for about 10 minutes, or until the carrot and pumpkin pieces are easily pierced with a fork.

Transfer the carrot, peach, and pumpkin to a blender (or food processor) with the remaining cooking liquid and blend until smooth.

STORAGE INFORMATION
3 days refrigerator
2 months freezer

carrot, pear, and sweet potato puree

2 large carrots, peeled and cut into ½- to ¾-inch slices (about 1¼ cups)

1 medium pear, peeled, cored, and sliced (½ to ¾ cup)

1 small sweet potato, peeled and cut into ½- to ¾-inch cubes (about 1 cup)

This is one of my son's favorite purees and one of my favorites to make! The ingredients are easy to find, but sometimes after a trip to the farmers' market in the fall, I'll substitute an apple for the pear. The flavors in this puree are nice and mild, as are the ingredients on your little one's tummy!

water level

COOKING TIME: 25 minutes

Pour water into the tank to the highest level (mine is level 3, which equals about 1 cup water).

Put the carrot, pear, and sweet potato in the steamer basket or cooking compartment.

Start the cooking process. When the cooking process is done, pour the carrot, pear, and sweet potato into the blending bowl with the cooking liquid. Blend.

fillable tank

COOKING TIME: 25 minutes

Fill the water tank with water.

Place the carrot, pear, and sweet potato into the blending bowl.

Set the steam timer for 25 minutes. When the timer goes off, blend the carrot, pear, and sweet potato with the cooking liquid.

stovetop

COOKING TIME: 13 minutes

In a 2-quart saucepan set over high heat, bring 1 cup water to a boil, about 3 minutes. Add the carrot, pear, and sweet potato; reduce the heat to medium-low; and place a tight-fitting lid on the saucepan. Steam for about 10 minutes, or until the carrot and sweet potato pieces are easily pierced with a fork.

Transfer the carrot, pear, and sweet potato to a blender (or food processor) with the remaining cooking liquid and blend until smooth.

STORAGE INFORMATION
3 days refrigerator
2 months freezer

cauliflower, plum, and date puree

1 cup cauliflower florets

1 medium plum, pitted and cut into slices (about ½ cup)

1 Medjool date, pitted and quartered lengthwise

In this recipe you're introducing dates to your little one. Sweet Medjool dates are great in this puree with cauliflower and plums. The color is a mild brown with pink tones from the plum, but don't let that discourage you from making this. It's delicious!

water level

COOKING TIME: 25 minutes

Pour water into the tank to the highest level (mine is level 3, which equals about 1 cup water).

Put the cauliflower, plum, and date in the steamer basket or cooking compartment.

Start the cooking process. When the cooking process is done, pour the cauliflower, plum, and date into the blending bowl with the cooking liquid. Blend.

fillable tank

COOKING TIME: 25 minutes

Fill the water tank with water.

Place the cauliflower, plum, and date into the blending bowl.

Set the steam timer for 25 minutes. When the timer goes off, blend the cauliflower, plum, and date with the cooking liquid.

stovetop

COOKING TIME: 13 minutes

In a 2-quart saucepan set over high heat, bring 1 cup water to a boil, about 3 minutes. Add the cauliflower, plum, and date; reduce the heat to medium-low; and place a tight-fitting lid on the saucepan. Steam for about 10 minutes, or until the cauliflower florets are easily pierced with a fork.

Transfer the cauliflower, plum, and date to a blender (or food processor) with the remaining cooking liquid and blend until smooth.

NOTE: Medjool dates are a dried fruit, so they need the cooking time to soften. If your date is particularly hard, put the dried fruit in a bowl and pour in enough boiling water just to cover. Cover the bowl and allow the fruit to soak up the water until plump and softened, then drain the water and proceed as above.

STORAGE INFORMATION
3 days refrigerator
2 months freezer

corn, pear, and cauliflower puree

1 cup fresh or frozen corn kernels

1 medium pear, peeled, cored, and cut into pieces (½ to ¾ cup)

1 cup cauliflower florets

I love purees with corn in them, as they remind me of sweet corn in the summertime. Always in abundant supply at the farmers' markets, this vegetable is also readily available in the freezer section during the cold months. When mixed with pear and cauliflower, it becomes a soft yellow color.

water level

COOKING TIME: 25 minutes

Pour water into the tank to the highest level (mine is level 3, which equals about 1 cup water).

Put the corn, pear, and cauliflower in the steamer basket or cooking compartment.

Start the cooking process. When the cooking process is done, pour the corn, pear, and cauliflower into the blending bowl with the cooking liquid. Blend.

fillable tank

COOKING TIME: 20 minutes

Fill the water tank with water.

Place the corn, pear, and cauliflower in the blending bowl.

Set the steam timer for 20 minutes. When the timer goes off, blend the corn, pear, and cauliflower with the cooking liquid.

stovetop

COOKING TIME: 13 minutes

In a 2-quart saucepan set over high heat, bring 1 cup water to a boil, about 3 minutes. Add the corn, pear, and cauliflower; reduce the heat to medium-low; and place a tight-fitting lid on the saucepan.

Steam for about 10 minutes, or until the cauliflower florets are easily pierced with a fork.

Transfer the corn, pear, and cauliflower to a blender (or food processor) with the remaining cooking liquid and blend until smooth.

STORAGE INFORMATION
3 days refrigerator
2 months freezer

green bean, kale, and pea puree

1 cup (1-inch) fresh or frozen trimmed green beans (about 6 ounces)

½ cup torn kale or spinach

½ cup fresh or frozen peas

This fiber-, folate-, and mineral-rich puree is a great way to introduce green beans to your little one. After trying green beans in this puree, my son has loved anything with green beans! In this recipe, I use fresh or frozen green beans.

water level

COOKING TIME: 25 minutes

Pour water into the tank to the highest level (mine is level 3, which equals about 1 cup water).

Put the green beans, kale, and peas in the steamer basket or cooking compartment.

Start the cooking process. When the cooking process is done, pour the green beans, kale, and peas into the blending bowl with the cooking liquid. Blend.

fillable tank

COOKING TIME: 15 minutes

Fill the water tank with water.

Place the green beans, kale, and peas into the blending bowl.

Set the steam timer for 15 minutes. When the timer goes off, blend the green beans, kale, and peas with the cooking liquid.

stovetop

COOKING TIME: 13 minutes

In a 2-quart saucepan set over high heat, bring 1 cup water to a boil, about 3 minutes. Add the green beans, kale, and peas; reduce the heat to medium-low; and place a tight-fitting lid on the saucepan. Steam for about 10 minutes, or until the green beans are easily pierced with a fork.

Transfer the green beans, kale, and peas to a blender (or food processor) with the remaining cooking liquid and blend until smooth.

STORAGE INFORMATION
3 days refrigerator
2 months freezer

green bean and squash puree

1 cup (1-inch) fresh or frozen trimmed green beans (about 6 ounces)

1 cup peeled, seeded, and cubed winter squash

Green beans and squash remind me of Thanksgiving! This puree would be great with a dash of nutmeg or cinnamon. If you don't have winter squash on hand, use sweet potato; they are interchangeable in this recipe.

water level
COOKING TIME: 25 minutes

Pour water into the tank to the highest level (mine is level 3, which equals about 1 cup water).

Put the green beans and squash in the steamer basket or cooking compartment.

Start the cooking process. When the cooking process is done, pour the green beans and squash into the blending bowl with the cooking liquid. Blend.

fillable tank
COOKING TIME: 25 minutes

Fill the water tank with water.

Place the green beans and squash in the blending bowl.

Set the steam timer for 25 minutes. When the timer goes off, blend the green beans and squash with the cooking liquid.

stovetop
COOKING TIME: 13 minutes

In a 2-quart saucepan set over high heat, bring 1 cup water to a boil, about 3 minutes. Add the green beans and squash, reduce the heat to medium-low, and place a tight-fitting lid on the saucepan. Steam for about 10 minutes, or until the green beans and squash cubes are easily pierced with a fork.

Transfer the green beans and squash to a blender (or food processor) with the remaining cooking liquid and blend until smooth.

STORAGE INFORMATION
3 days refrigerator
2 months freezer

mango, pineapple, and pumpkin puree

1 cup peeled, pitted, and sliced fresh mango or frozen mango pieces

½ cup peeled and cubed pineapple

½ cup (½- to ¾-inch cubes) peeled and cleaned pumpkin

Mangoes and pineapple are super sweet all by themselves, so the pumpkin in this puree helps balance that sweetness. This beautiful orange puree is high in vitamin C and can easily be made into a smoothie. I like making a double batch and freezing the puree in an ice cube tray. Then, in the morning, I toss the cubes into a blender with unsweetened almond milk and, voilà, a morning smoothie (see page 218)! If you don't have any pumpkin, you can substitute sweet potato.

water level
COOKING TIME: 25 minutes

Pour water into the tank to the highest level (mine is level 3, which equals about 1 cup water).

Put the mango, pineapple, and pumpkin in the steamer basket or cooking compartment.

Start the cooking process. When the cooking process is done, pour the mango, pineapple, and pumpkin into the blending bowl with the cooking liquid. Blend.

fillable tank
COOKING TIME: 25 minutes

Fill the water tank with water.

Place the mango, pineapple, and pumpkin in the blending bowl.

Set the steam timer for 25 minutes. When the timer goes off, blend the mango, pineapple, and pumpkin with the cooking liquid.

stovetop
COOKING TIME: 13 minutes

In a 2-quart saucepan set over high heat, bring 1 cup water to a boil, about 3 minutes. Add the mango, pineapple, and pumpkin; reduce the heat to medium-low; and place a tight-fitting lid on the saucepan. Steam for about 10 minutes, or until the pumpkin cubes are easily pierced with a fork.

Transfer the mango, pineapple, and pumpkin to a blender (or food processor) with the remaining cooking liquid and blend until smooth.

STORAGE INFORMATION
3 days refrigerator
2 months freezer

nectarine, peach, and sweet potato puree

1 medium nectarine, peeled, pitted, and cut into large slices (about ½ cup)

1 medium peach, peeled, pitted, and cut into large slices (about ½ cup)

1 cup (½- to ¾-inch cubes) peeled sweet potato

Nectarine and peaches are both delicious stone fruits that blend with sweet potato to make a sweet and tart puree. When first introducing nectarine and peach, I recommend peeling the skin so the puree is even smoother, but after baby has had the puree a few times, feel free to leave the skin on.

water level
COOKING TIME: 25 minutes

Pour water into the tank to the highest level (mine is level 3, which equals about 1 cup water).

Put the nectarine, peach, and sweet potato in the steamer basket or cooking compartment.

Start the cooking process. When the cooking process is done, pour the nectarine, peach, and sweet potato into the blending bowl with the cooking liquid. Blend.

fillable tank
COOKING TIME: 25 minutes

Fill the water tank with water.

Place the nectarine, peach, and sweet potato in the blending bowl.

Set the steam timer for 25 minutes. When the timer goes off, blend the nectarine, peach, and sweet potato with the cooking liquid.

stovetop
COOKING TIME: 13 minutes

In a 2-quart saucepan set over high heat, bring 1 cup water to a boil, about 3 minutes. Add the nectarine, peach, and sweet potato; reduce the heat to medium-low; and place a tight-fitting lid on the saucepan. Steam for 10 minutes, or until the sweet potato cubes are easily pierced with a fork.

Transfer the nectarine, peach, and sweet potato to a blender (or food processor) with the cooking liquid and blend.

STORAGE INFORMATION
3 days refrigerator
2 months freezer

winter and summer squash puree

1 cup (½- to ¾-inch cubes) peeled and seeded winter squash

1 cup chopped unpeeled summer squash

In this puree, winter and summer squash are combined. On its own, summer squash (zucchini or yellow squash) can be watery, but when blended with hearty winter squash (butternut or acorn squash), you're left with a silky smooth golden puree baby will love.

water level
COOKING TIME: 25 minutes

Pour water into the tank to the highest level (mine is level 3, which equals about 1 cup water).

Put the squash in the steamer basket or cooking compartment.

Start the cooking process. When the cooking process is done, pour the squash into the blending bowl with the cooking liquid. Blend.

fillable tank
COOKING TIME: 25 minutes

Fill the water tank with water.

Place the squash in the blending bowl.

Set the steam timer for 25 minutes. When the timer goes off, blend the squash with the cooking liquid.

stovetop
COOKING TIME: 15 minutes

In a 2-quart saucepan, bring 1 cup water to a boil, about 3 minutes. Add the squash, reduce the heat to medium-low, and place a tight-fitting lid on the saucepan. Steam for 10 to 12 minutes, until the winter squash cubes are easily pierced with a fork.

Transfer the squash to a blender (or food processor) with the remaining water and blend.

STORAGE INFORMATION
3 days refrigerator
2 months freezer

baby "cereals" and grains

½ cup grains (brown rice, oats, barley, or quinoa)

It's so easy to make homemade versions of the baby cereals that you usually purchase at the store! Want to know how easy it is? Just grind brown rice or any type of oats, and the end result is brown rice cereal or oatmeal for babies!

A batch of whole grains prepared and stored ready for use can be a fantastic meal for both baby and you! Use grains with Berry, Date, and Chia Seed Puree (page 108) for a breakfast bowl, or try some Secretly Carrot Cheddar Cheese Sauce (page 155) on top of grains for a hearty lunch or dinner.

What's great about grains is that they are so interchangeable. Don't have quinoa in the house? Not a problem; use brown rice.

Note that while the baby food maker blending feature is great for blending and pureeing steamed food, it doesn't quite have the power to grind hard whole grains like brown rice into the fine, powdery consistency you want. It will grind up oats, but for most other grains, I'd recommend a blender, food processor, or spice grinder.

Place the grains in a blender, food processor, or spice grinder and blend at high speed until finely ground, about 30 seconds.

Store the ground grains in an airtight container in a cool, dark place (like the refrigerator) for up to 2 months.

To make a serving of brown rice, barley, or quinoa grain cereal for baby: In a 2-quart saucepan over medium-high heat, bring ½ cup water (about ½ inch) to a slow boil, about 2 minutes. Pour in 2 tablespoons ground cereal and turn off the heat. Stir so that no lumps form, and stir a few more times over the next 3 to 4 minutes, until the cereal is thick.

To make a serving of oatmeal cereal for baby: In a bowl, stir ¼ cup warm water, breast milk, or formula with 2 tablespoons ground oat cereal until blended. If it's too thick, add a few more teaspoons of warm liquid until the desired consistency is reached.

STORAGE INFORMATION
3 days refrigerator
2 months freezer

introducing meat, poultry, and fish purees

1 to 2 ounces cubed meat, poultry, or fish (peeled, deveined, and tails removed if using shrimp or fish)

½ cup peeled and cubed sweet potato

¼ cup no-sodium beef, chicken, or vegetable broth

Meat, poultry, and fish are good sources of iron and protein. The key to an agreeable and palatable meat, poultry, or fish puree is combining it with a fruit or vegetable your baby has had before, or even with an herb or spice your baby is familiar with and likes, and then make the texture smooth enough so baby can try it out.

water level
COOKING TIME: 25 minutes

Pour water into the tank to the highest level (mine is level 3, which equals about 1 cup water).

Place the protein and the sweet potato in the steamer basket or cooking compartment. Pour in the broth.

Start the cooking process. When the cooking process is done, pour the contents of the steamer basket into the blending bowl with the cooking liquid. Blend.

fillable tank
COOKING TIME: 20 minutes

Fill the water tank with water.

Place the meat and sweet potato in the blending bowl and pour in the broth.

Set the steam timer for 20 minutes. When the timer goes off, blend the contents of the blending bowl.

stovetop
COOKING TIME: 13 minutes

In a 2-quart saucepan set over high heat, bring 1 cup water to a boil, about 3 minutes. Add the protein and sweet potato, pour in the broth, reduce the heat to medium-low, and place a tight-fitting lid on the saucepan. Steam for 10 minutes, or until the protein is cooked through (145°F for meat and fish, 165°F for poultry) and the sweet potato cubes are easily pierced with a fork.

Transfer the contents of the saucepan to a blender (or food processor) and blend until smooth.

NOTES: If the puree is too thick, add a little bit of liquid (breast milk, formula, or water) to reach the desired consistency.

Feel free to use herbs and spices too. I like to add fresh or dried thyme or parsley (½ teaspoon dried, or 1½ teaspoons fresh) before blending.

When shopping for meat or poultry, you'll encounter numerous labels (USDA Prime, All Natural, etc.), but the two most important to look for are Organic and either Grass Fed (beef) or Free Range (poultry). You want to make sure the ingredients you buy are grass fed or free range *and* organic, because they contain superior nutritional content and taste better than their grain-diet counterparts.

STORAGE INFORMATION
2 days refrigerator
2 months freezer

chunky purees

TYPICALLY 6 TO 9 MONTHS

Once baby has eaten combination ingredient purees,
you have a lot more building blocks to play with: spices,
herbs, dairy, and meat. And the puree can be chunkier
as baby starts to explore textures.

I'll never forget introducing herbs and spices to my
baby. Not only did it become more fun to cook for him
and make new flavor combinations he'd love, but he
also seemed to really enjoy trying new flavors—
and he still does to this day!

After one of my sisters-in-law saw my son trying
cinnamon one day, turmeric the next, she joked that he
has a more sophisticated palate than she does.
It's all about experimenting and getting them to try
new flavors. If they don't like a particular herb or spice,
that's okay; try again in a few days.

It's good to leave the purees in this chapter a little thicker and chunkier so baby experiences new textures. But, as before, if a puree is a bit too thick, just add a little water, formula, or breast milk to reach the desired consistency.

Sweet Potato, Coconut Milk, and Curry Puree 91

Sweet Potato, Squash, and Cinnamon Puree 93

Apple, Pear, and Cinnamon Puree 94

Spinach, Pea, and Basil Puree 95

Pumpkin, Apple, and Nutmeg Puree 96

Banana, Berry, and Grain Puree 97

Carrot, Orange, Nutmeg, and Ginger Puree 98

Pumpkin, Mango, and Turmeric Puree 99

Apricot, Spinach, Zucchini, and Brown Rice Puree 100

Spinach, Zucchini, Quinoa, and Cumin Puree 102

Sweet Potato, Raisin, Cinnamon, and Quinoa Puree 103

Apple, Cinnamon, Raisin, and Quinoa Puree 105

Parsnip, Onion, Squash, and Coconut Milk Puree 106

Swiss Chard, Beet, Mango, and Cinnamon Puree 107

Berry, Date, and Chia Seed Puree 108

Banana, Oat, Sweet Potato, and Allspice Puree 110

Beet, Squash, and Yogurt Puree 111

Peach, Plum, Pepper, and Grain Puree 113

Eggplant, Berry, and Grain Puree 114

Berry, Quinoa, and Yogurt Puree 115

Beef, Avocado, and Black Bean Puree 116

Chicken, Squash, and Potato Puree 119

Chicken, Kale, and Quinoa Puree 120

Chicken, Pea, and Pear Puree 121

Pork, Sweet Potato, and Apple Puree 122

Salmon, Sweet Potato, and Apple Puree 123

Fish, Garlic, and Cauliflower Puree 124

Tofu, Carrot, and Cauliflower Puree 125

Tofu, Squash, and Green Bean Puree 126

Tofu, Sweet Potato, and Turmeric Puree 128

Lentil, Pepper, and Sweet Potato Puree 129

Banana, Mango, Pear, and Coconut Milk Puree 130

Mango, Banana, Cauliflower, and Spinach Puree 131

Pineapple, Sweet Potato, and Ginger Puree 132

Berry, Avocado, and Coconut Milk Puree 133

Beet, Apple, and Watermelon Puree 134

Peach, Nectarine, and Mango Puree 135

sweet potato, coconut milk, and curry puree

1 medium sweet potato, peeled and cut into ½- to ¾-inch cubes (about 1 cup)

¼ cup full-fat coconut milk, plus more as needed

¼ teaspoon curry powder

Sweet potatoes are a great "base" when you're introducing spices. The one I've used here, curry, brings out the subtle sweetness of sweet potatoes. Coconut milk is thick and creamy, and it introduces a good plant-based saturated fat to baby's diet.

water level
COOKING TIME: 25 minutes

Pour water into the tank to the highest level (mine is level 3, which equals about 1 cup water).

Put the sweet potato in the steamer basket or cooking compartment and pour in the coconut milk as well; it will go through the steamer basket into the blending bowl (or you can pour the coconut milk directly into the blending bowl before inserting the steamer basket).

Start the cooking process. When the cooking process is done, pour the sweet potato into the blending bowl with the coconut milk and cooking liquid, add the curry powder, and blend.

fillable tank
COOKING TIME: 25 minutes

Fill the water tank with water.

Place the sweet potato into the blending bowl and pour the coconut milk into the blending bowl as well.

Set the steam timer for 25 minutes. When the timer goes off, add the curry powder and blend.

stovetop
COOKING TIME: 14 minutes

In a 2-quart saucepan set over high heat, bring ½ cup water to a boil, about 2 minutes. Add the sweet potato and the coconut milk, reduce the heat to medium-low, and place a tight-fitting lid on the saucepan. Steam for 10 to 12 minutes, until the sweet potato cubes are easily pierced with a fork.

Transfer the sweet potato to a blender (or food processor) with the coconut milk and cooking liquid, add the curry powder, and blend.

STORAGE INFORMATION
3 days refrigerator
2 months freezer

NOTE: If the puree is too thick, add a teaspoon or more of coconut milk to reach the desired consistency.

sweet potato, squash, and cinnamon puree

1 cup (½- to ¾-inch cubes) unpeeled sweet potato

1 cup peeled, seeded, and cubed butternut or acorn squash

¼ teaspoon ground cinnamon

Cinnamon was one of the first spices I introduced to my son. Sweet potatoes and winter squash are a perfect vehicle for a little spice. Winter squash has an almost sweet, earthy orange flesh. This puree can be made with an additional touch of grated nutmeg and vanilla extract (see Note), and it ends up tasting like a pie filling (leave out the sugar for baby).

water level

COOKING TIME: 25 minutes

Pour water into the tank to the highest level (mine is level 3, which equals about 1 cup water).

Put the sweet potato and squash in the steamer basket or cooking compartment.

Start the cooking process. When the cooking process is done, pour the sweet potato and squash into the blending bowl with the cooking liquid, add the cinnamon, and blend.

fillable tank

COOKING TIME: 25 minutes

Fill the water tank with water.

Place the sweet potato and squash in the blending bowl.

Set the steam timer for 25 minutes. When the timer goes off, add the cinnamon and blend.

stovetop

COOKING TIME: 13 minutes

In a 2-quart saucepan set over high heat, bring 1 cup water to a boil, about 3 minutes. Add the sweet potato and squash, reduce the heat to medium-low, and place a tight-fitting lid on the saucepan. Steam for about 10 minutes, or until the sweet potato and squash cubes are easily pierced with a fork.

Transfer the sweet potato and squash to a blender (or food processor) with the cooking liquid, add the cinnamon, and blend.

NOTE: This puree is great with a dash of freshly grated nutmeg and ½ teaspoon pure vanilla extract added along with the cinnamon.

STORAGE INFORMATION
3 days refrigerator
2 months freezer

apple, pear, and cinnamon puree

1 medium apple, peeled, cored, and cut into chunks (about 1 cup)

1 medium pear, peeled, cored, and cut into pieces (about 1 cup)

½ teaspoon ground cinnamon

Apple and pear with cinnamon is the fall flavor trifecta. This is one combination that I make all the time, and it tastes better than any store-bought applesauce I've ever had! This apple-pear-cinnamon puree is also great in yogurt breakfast parfaits (see page 183).

water level
COOKING TIME: 25 minutes

Pour water into the tank to the highest level (mine is level 3, which equals about 1 cup water).

Put the apple and pear in the steamer basket or cooking compartment.

Start the cooking process. When the cooking process is done, drain and discard the cooking liquid. Pour the apple and pear into the blending bowl, add the cinnamon, and blend.

fillable tank
COOKING TIME: 20 minutes

Fill the water tank with water.

Place the apple and pear in the blending bowl.

Set the steam timer for 20 minutes. When the timer goes off, drain and discard the cooking liquid. Add the cinnamon to the blending bowl and blend.

stovetop
COOKING TIME: 13 minutes

In a 2-quart saucepan set over high heat, bring 1 cup water to a boil, about 3 minutes. Add the apple and pear, reduce the heat to medium-low, and place a tight-fitting lid on the saucepan. Steam for about 10 minutes, or until the apple chunks are easily pierced with a fork. Drain off and discard the cooking liquid.

Transfer the apple and pear to a blender (or food processor), add the cinnamon, and blend.

STORAGE INFORMATION
3 days refrigerator
2 months freezer

spinach, pea, and basil puree

1 cup baby spinach leaves

1 cup fresh or frozen peas

2 fresh medium basil leaves, or ½ teaspoon dried

I love cooking with basil because the aromatic herb makes the whole kitchen smell fresh, just like summertime. This is one of those purees that can be made with fresh ingredients or with frozen peas and dried basil in a pinch. This versatile puree can also be used as a sauce for chicken and rice!

water level

COOKING TIME: 17 minutes

Pour water into the tank to the middle level (mine is level 2, which equals about ⅔ cup water).

Put the spinach and peas in the steamer basket or cooking compartment.

Start the cooking process. When the cooking process is done, pour the spinach and peas in the blending bowl with the cooking liquid and add the basil. Blend.

fillable tank

COOKING TIME: 15 minutes

Fill the water tank with water.

Place the spinach and peas into the blending bowl.

Set the steam timer for 15 minutes. When the timer goes off, add the basil and blend.

stovetop

COOKING TIME: 7 minutes

In a 2-quart saucepan set over high heat, bring ½ cup water to a boil, about 2 minutes. Add the spinach and peas, reduce the heat to medium-low, and place a tight-fitting lid on the saucepan. Steam for about 5 minutes, or until the peas are easily pierced with a fork.

Transfer the spinach and peas to a blender (or food processor) with the remaining cooking liquid, add the basil, and blend.

NOTE: I add fresh basil at the end because it tends to be more flavorful, plus it stays greener!

STORAGE INFORMATION
3 days refrigerator
2 months freezer

pumpkin, apple, and nutmeg puree

1 apple, peeled, cored, and cut into chunks (about 1 cup)

1 cup peeled and cubed pumpkin

¼ teaspoon freshly grated nutmeg

If autumn came in puree form, it would be this one: apples, pumpkins, and nutmeg—cozy fall ingredients all mixed together. I usually make a double or triple batch of this to freeze so I always have some on hand.

water level
COOKING TIME: 25 minutes

Pour water into the tank to the highest level (mine is level 3, which equals about 1 cup water).

Put the apple and pumpkin in the steamer basket or cooking compartment.

Start the cooking process. When the cooking process is done, drain and discard the cooking liquid. Pour the apple and pumpkin into the blending bowl, add the nutmeg, and blend.

fillable tank
COOKING TIME: 25 minutes

Fill the water tank with water.

Place the apple and pumpkin in the blending bowl.

Set the steam timer for 25 minutes. When the timer goes off, drain and discard the cooking liquid. Add the nutmeg to the blending bowl and blend.

stovetop
COOKING TIME: 13 minutes

In a 2-quart saucepan set over high heat, bring 1 cup water to a boil, about 3 minutes. Add the apple and pumpkin, reduce the heat to medium-low, and place a tight-fitting lid on the saucepan. Steam for about 10 minutes, or until the apple and pumpkin cubes are easily pierced with a fork. Drain and discard the cooking liquid.

Transfer the apple and pumpkin to a blender (or food processor), add the nutmeg, and blend.

NOTE: A little nutmeg goes a long way. You don't want to overpower this puree, so start with ¼ teaspoon, or a generous pinch, and go up from there if you think it needs a little more.

STORAGE INFORMATION
3 days refrigerator
2 months freezer

banana, berry, and grain puree

½ medium banana, peeled and cut into 1-inch pieces

2 strawberries, hulled and cut into pieces, or 6 raspberries, blueberries, or blackberries (or a combination)

1 serving prepared baby cereal or oatmeal (see page 86)

This great breakfast food has an almost pie-like taste! I love making this puree with banana and strawberries, but you could instead use mixed berries. I make the banana berry sauce and then swirl it on top of warm cereal for a healthy breakfast.

water level
COOKING TIME: 10 minutes

Pour water into the tank to the lowest level (mine is level 1, which equals about ⅓ cup water).

Put the banana and berries in the steamer basket or cooking compartment.

Start the cooking process. When the cooking process is done, pour the banana and strawberries into the blending bowl with the cooking liquid. Blend.

Pour the berry sauce over the prepared cereal and stir to combine.

fillable tank
COOKING TIME: 5 minutes

Fill the water tank with water.

Place the banana and berries into the blending bowl.

Set the steam timer for 5 minutes. When the timer goes off, blend the banana and berries with the cooking liquid.

Pour the berry sauce over the prepared cereal and stir to combine.

stovetop
COOKING TIME: 4 minutes

In a 2-quart saucepan set over high heat, bring ½ cup water to a boil, about 2 minutes. Add the banana and berries, reduce the heat to medium-low, and place a tight-fitting lid on the saucepan. Steam for 2 minutes.

Transfer the banana and berries to a blender (or food processor) with the remaining cooking liquid and blend.

Pour the berry sauce over the prepared cereal and stir to combine.

NOTE: Instead of oatmeal, you could use another cooked grain (like quinoa or brown rice). This puree can be divided into two containers and served on different days.

STORAGE INFORMATION
3 days refrigerator
2 months freezer

carrot, orange, nutmeg, and ginger puree

3 large carrots, peeled and cut into ½-inch slices (about 2 cups)

¼ cup fresh orange juice, plus more as needed (see Note)

½ teaspoon peeled and grated fresh ginger, or a small pinch of ground ginger

¼ teaspoon freshly grated nutmeg

Fall and winter are seasons you want to enjoy with a nice latte and a cozy sweater, not a sick baby! This immunity-boosting puree will help keep them healthy all season long! Ginger has antibacterial properties and is anti-inflammatory and also great for the immune system. This puree makes a wonderful side dish—think of it as an alternative to mashed potatoes. Just add a tablespoon of butter and top it with fresh snipped chives!

water level

COOKING TIME: 25 minutes

Pour water into the tank to the highest level (mine is level 3, which equals about 1 cup water).

Put the carrot in the steamer basket or cooking compartment and pour in the orange juice; it will go through the steamer basket into the blending bowl (or you could pour the orange juice directly into the blending bowl before inserting the steamer basket).

Start the cooking process. When the cooking process is done, pour the carrot into the blending bowl with the cooking liquid and orange juice, add the ginger and nutmeg, and blend. If the puree is too thick, add a teaspoon or more of orange juice to reach the desired consistency.

fillable tank

COOKING TIME: 25 minutes

Fill the water tank with water.

Place the carrot in the blending bowl and pour the orange juice into the blending bowl as well.

Set the steam timer for 25 minutes. When the timer goes off, add the ginger and nutmeg and blend. If the puree is too thick, add a teaspoon or more of orange juice to reach the desired consistency.

stovetop

COOKING TIME: 14 minutes

In a 2-quart saucepan set over high heat, bring ½ cup water to a boil, about 2 minutes. Add the carrot and orange juice, reduce the heat to medium-low, and place a tight-fitting lid on the saucepan. Steam for 10 to 12 minutes, or until the carrot slices are easily pierced with a fork.

Transfer the contents of the saucepan to a blender (or food processor) with the cooking liquid, add the ginger and nutmeg, and blend. If the puree is too thick, add a teaspoon or more of orange juice to reach the desired consistency.

STORAGE INFORMATION
3 days refrigerator
2 months freezer

NOTES: Omit the orange juice and instead peel an orange and steam half the orange flesh with the carrots before blending.

pumpkin, mango, and turmeric puree

1 cup peeled, pitted, and sliced fresh mango or frozen mango pieces

1 cup (½- to ¾-inch cubes) peeled and cleaned pumpkin

¼ teaspoon ground turmeric

Adding mango and a pinch of turmeric to pumpkin gives this puree a tropical feel. If you don't have pumpkin on hand, you can use butternut squash or sweet potatoes. You won't taste the turmeric because of the strong mango flavor, but it's included for the added health benefits it provides. Serve this with yogurt and some granola either as a snack or as breakfast for mom!

water level
COOKING TIME: 25 minutes

Pour water into the tank to the highest level (mine is level 3, which equals about 1 cup water).

Put the mango and pumpkin in the steamer basket or cooking compartment.

Start the cooking process. When the cooking process is done, drain and discard a little of the cooking liquid (or all of it for a thicker puree). Pour the mango, pumpkin, and remaining cooking liquid into the blending bowl and add the turmeric. Blend.

fillable tank
COOKING TIME: 20 minutes

Fill the water tank with water.

Place the mango and pumpkin in the blending bowl.

Set the steam timer for 20 minutes. When the timer goes off, drain and discard a little of the cooking liquid (or all of it for a thicker puree). Add the turmeric to the blending bowl and blend.

stovetop
COOKING TIME: 13 minutes

In a 2-quart saucepan set over high heat, bring 1 cup water to a boil, about 3 minutes. Add the mango and pumpkin, reduce the heat to medium-low, and place a tight-fitting lid on the saucepan. Steam for about 10 minutes, or until the pumpkin cubes are easily pierced with a fork. Drain and discard a little of the cooking liquid (or all of it for a thicker puree).

Transfer the mango and pumpkin to a blender (or food processor) with the remaining cooking liquid, add the turmeric, and blend.

NOTE: Add ¼ teaspoon grated fresh ginger and ½ cup pineapple cubes and turn this into a smoothie (see page 218), or serve the puree over yogurt and top with granola.

STORAGE INFORMATION
3 days refrigerator
2 months freezer

apricot, spinach, zucchini, and brown rice puree

1 apricot, pitted and cut into large pieces

½ cup chopped baby spinach

1 cup chopped unpeeled zucchini

¼ cup cooked brown rice

Apricot makes this otherwise green and slightly bland puree come to life. Although it's on the milder side, apricot, spinach, and zucchini combined with brown rice offer baby a good mix of fruit, vegetable, and grain.

water level
COOKING TIME: 25 minutes

Pour water into the tank to the highest level (mine is level 3, which equals about 1 cup water).

Put the apricot, spinach, and zucchini in the steamer basket or cooking compartment.

Start the cooking process. When the cooking process is done, drain and discard a little of the cooking liquid (or all of it for a thicker puree). Pour the apricot, spinach, and zucchini into the blending bowl with the remaining cooking liquid and add the brown rice. Blend.

fillable tank
COOKING TIME: 20 minutes

Fill the water tank with water.

Place the apricot, spinach, and zucchini in the blending bowl.

Set the steam timer for 20 minutes. When the timer goes off, drain and discard a little of the cooking liquid (or all of it for a thicker puree). Add the brown rice to the blending bowl and blend.

stovetop
COOKING TIME: 11 minutes

In a small 2-quart saucepan set over high heat, bring 1 cup water (about 1 inch) to a boil, about 3 minutes. Add the apricot, spinach, and zucchini; reduce the heat to medium-low; and place a tight-fitting lid on the saucepan. Steam for about 8 minutes, or until the zucchini pieces are easily pierced with a fork. Drain off and discard a little of the cooking liquid (or all of it for a thicker puree).

Transfer the apricot, spinach, and zucchini to a blender (or food processor) with the remaining cooking liquid, add the cooked brown rice, and blend.

STORAGE INFORMATION
3 days refrigerator
2 months freezer

NOTE: This puree is great with a pinch of a savory herb, like thyme, oregano, or rosemary, either fresh or dried, stirred in at either the beginning or end of cooking.

spinach, zucchini, quinoa, and cumin puree

1 cup chopped baby spinach

1 cup chopped unpeeled zucchini

¼ cup cooked quinoa

¼ teaspoon ground cumin

Cumin adds a nice mild favor to this puree. In place of or in addition to cumin, a savory fresh or dried herb could be used, stirred in at the end; my favorites for this puree are thyme, basil, parsley, and rosemary.

water level
COOKING TIME: 25 minutes

Pour water into the tank to the highest level (mine is level 3, which equals about 1 cup water).

Put the spinach and zucchini in the steamer basket or cooking compartment.

Start the cooking process. When the cooking process is done, drain and discard a little of the cooking liquid (or all of it for a thicker puree). Pour the spinach and zucchini into the blending bowl with the remaining cooking liquid, add the cooked quinoa and cumin, and blend.

fillable tank
COOKING TIME: 20 minutes

Fill the water tank with water.

Place the spinach and zucchini in the blending bowl.

Set the steam timer for 20 minutes. When the timer goes off, drain and discard a little of the cooking liquid (or all of it for a thicker puree). Add the cooked quinoa and cumin to the blending bowl and blend.

stovetop
COOKING TIME: 11 minutes

In a 2-quart saucepan set over high heat, bring 1 cup water to a boil, about 3 minutes. Add the spinach and zucchini, reduce the heat to medium-low, and place a tight-fitting lid on the saucepan. Steam for about 8 minutes, or until the zucchini pieces are easily pierced with a fork. Drain and discard a little of the cooking liquid (or all of it for a thicker puree).

Transfer the spinach and zucchini to a blender (or food processor) with the remaining cooking liquid, add the cooked quinoa and cumin, and blend.

STORAGE INFORMATION
3 days refrigerator
2 months freezer

sweet potato, raisin, cinnamon, and quinoa puree

1½ cups peeled and cubed sweet potato

2 tablespoons raisins

¼ teaspoon ground cinnamon

¼ cup cooked quinoa

Raisins and cinnamon add such a sweet and warming flavor (and smell) when you're making baby foods. This puree is especially wonderful in early fall, when sweet potatoes are in abundance at the farmers' market and you want a nice warm and hearty puree for your little one.

water level
COOKING TIME: 25 minutes

Pour water into the tank to the highest level (mine is level 3, which equals about 1 cup water).

Put the sweet potato and raisins in the steamer basket or cooking compartment.

Start the cooking process. When the cooking process is done, drain and discard a little of the cooking liquid (or all of it for a thicker puree). Pour the sweet potato and raisins into the blending bowl with the remaining cooking liquid, add the cinnamon and cooked quinoa, and blend.

fillable tank
COOKING TIME: 20 minutes

Fill the water tank with water.

Place the sweet potato and raisins in the blending bowl.

Set the steam timer for 20 minutes. When the timer goes off, drain and discard a little of the cooking liquid (or all of it for a thicker puree). Add the cinnamon and cooked quinoa to the blending bowl and blend.

stovetop
COOKING TIME: 13 minutes

In a 2-quart saucepan set over high heat, bring 1 cup water to a boil, about 3 minutes. Add the sweet potato and raisins, reduce the heat to medium-low, and place a tight-fitting lid on the saucepan. Steam for about 10 minutes, or until the sweet potato cubes are easily pierced with a fork. Drain and discard a little of the cooking liquid (or all of it for a thicker puree).

Transfer the sweet potato and raisins to a blender (or food processor) with the remaining cooking liquid, add the cinnamon and cooked quinoa, and blend.

STORAGE INFORMATION
3 days refrigerator
2 months freezer

apple, cinnamon, raisin, and quinoa puree

1 medium apple, peeled, cored, and cut into chunks (about 1 cup)

¼ cup raisins

¼ teaspoon ground cinnamon

¼ cup cooked quinoa

I can tell you with absolute certainty that this was my son's favorite puree. With a smile on his face, he would wiggle and wave his little hands every time he'd get a spoonful. This puree is made by combining apples, raisins, and cinnamon and then adding cooked quinoa before pureeing it. It also has protein in it because of the quinoa!

water level
COOKING TIME: 25 minutes

Pour water into the tank to the highest level (mine is level 3, which equals about 1 cup water).

Put the apple and raisins in the steamer basket or cooking compartment.

Start the cooking process. When the cooking process is done, drain and discard a little of the cooking liquid (or all of it for a thicker puree). Pour the apple and raisins into the blending bowl with the remaining cooking liquid, add the cinnamon and cooked quinoa, and blend.

fillable tank
COOKING TIME: 20 minutes

Fill the water tank with water.

Place the apple and raisins in the blending bowl.

Set the steam timer for 20 minutes. When the timer goes off, drain and discard a little of the cooking liquid (or all of it for a thicker puree). Add the cinnamon and cooked quinoa to the blending bowl and blend.

stovetop
COOKING TIME: 13 minutes

In a 2-quart saucepan set over high heat, bring 1 cup water to a boil, about 3 minutes. Add the apple and raisins, reduce the heat to medium-low, and place a tight-fitting lid on the saucepan. Steam for about 10 minutes, or until the apple chunks are easily pierced with a fork. Drain and discard a little of the cooking liquid (or all of it for a thicker puree).

Transfer the apple and raisins to a blender (or food processor) with the remaining cooking liquid, add the cinnamon and cooked quinoa, and blend.

STORAGE INFORMATION
3 days refrigerator
2 months freezer

parsnip, onion, squash, and coconut milk puree

2 large parsnips, peeled and cut into ½-inch slices (about 1½ cups)

½ cup peeled, seeded, and cubed butternut squash

¼ cup finely chopped white or yellow onion

¼ cup full-fat coconut milk, plus more as needed

If it's served warm, this puree tastes like a wonderful autumnal root vegetable soup. Parsnips, a white root vegetable closely related to the carrot, mixes with the other ingredients here for a silky smooth texture. If you cannot find parsnips, feel free to use carrots. And if you do not have butternut squash on hand, you can use sweet potatoes.

water level

COOKING TIME: 25 minutes

Pour water into the tank to the highest level (mine is level 3, which equals about 1 cup water).

Put the parsnip, squash, and onion in the steamer basket or cooking compartment and pour in the coconut milk; it will go through the steamer basket or cooking compartment into the blending bowl (or you could pour the coconut milk directly into the blending bowl before inserting the steamer basket).

Start the cooking process. When the cooking process is done, pour the parsnip, squash, and onion into the blending bowl with the cooking liquid and coconut milk. Blend.

fillable tank

COOKING TIME: 25 minutes

Fill the water tank with water.

Place the parsnip, squash, and onion in the blending bowl and pour the coconut milk into the blending bowl as well.

Set the steam timer for 25 minutes. When the timer goes off, blend until smooth.

stovetop

COOKING TIME: 13 minutes

In a 2-quart saucepan set over high heat, bring 1 cup water to a boil, about 3 minutes. Add the parsnip, squash, and onion; pour in the coconut milk; reduce the heat to medium-low; and place a tight-fitting lid on the saucepan. Steam for 10 to 12 minutes, or until the vegetables are easily pierced with a fork.

Transfer the parsnip, squash, and onion to a blender (or food processor) with the remaining cooking liquid and coconut milk and blend.

NOTES: Curry powder or a bold spice like ground cumin or turmeric would be a great addition to this puree. Just add ¼ teaspoon of the powder or spice before blending.

If the puree is too thick, add a teaspoon or more of coconut milk to reach the desired consistency.

STORAGE INFORMATION
3 days refrigerator
2 months freezer

swiss chard, beet, mango, and cinnamon puree

1 cup chopped Swiss chard (about 3 leaves)

1 small beet, peeled and cut into small ½-inch cubes (about ½ cup)

½ cup peeled, pitted, and cubed mango

¼ teaspoon ground cinnamon

In the summertime, Swiss chard is always readily available at the farmers' market, and it deserves more attention than it gets. It is so beautiful: a big leafy green with white, yellow, or red stalks. The flavor is earthy and bold, and it tastes very similar to spinach and kale, so if you can't find Swiss chard, use kale or spinach instead. The mango, beets, and cinnamon add a mild, warm sweetness.

water level
COOKING TIME: 25 minutes

Pour water into the tank to the highest level (mine is level 3, which equals about 1 cup water).

Put the chard, beet, and mango in the steamer basket or cooking compartment.

Start the cooking process. When the cooking process is done, drain and discard a little of the cooking liquid (or all of it for a thicker puree). Pour the chard, beet, and mango into the blending bowl with the remaining cooking liquid, add the cinnamon, and blend.

fillable tank
COOKING TIME: 20 minutes

Fill the water tank with water.

Place the chard, beet, and mango in the blending bowl.

Set the steam timer for 20 minutes. When the timer goes off, drain and discard a little of the cooking liquid (or all of it for a thicker puree). Add the cinnamon to the blending bowl and blend.

stovetop
COOKING TIME: 13 minutes

In a 2-quart saucepan set over high heat, bring 1 cup water to a boil, about 3 minutes. Add the chard, beet, and mango; reduce the heat to medium-low; and place a tight-fitting lid on the saucepan. Steam for about 10 minutes, or until the beet cubes are easily pierced with a fork. Drain and discard a little of the cooking liquid (or all of it for a thicker puree).

Transfer the chard, beet, and mango to a blender (or food processor) with the remaining cooking liquid, add the cinnamon, and blend.

STORAGE INFORMATION
3 days refrigerator
2 months freezer

berry, date, and chia seed puree

1¼ cups raspberries, blueberries, blackberries, or a combination

1 Medjool date, pitted and diced

1 teaspoon chia seeds

Chia seeds have so many health benefits: they're high in fiber, protein, omega-3 fatty acids, calcium, magnesium, and phosphorus—among other nutrients. When mixed with a liquid, chia seeds plump up and take on a gelatinous texture, like a pudding, so don't worry if your puree gets a little thicker after it has been refrigerated. If you want a thinner puree, simply add a little more liquid and stir before serving.

water level
COOKING TIME: 17 minutes

Pour water into the tank to the medium level (mine is level 2, which equals about ⅔ cup water).

Put the berries and date in the steamer basket or cooking compartment and add the chia seeds.

Start the cooking process. When the cooking process is done, pour the berries, date, and chia seeds into the blending bowl with the cooking liquid. Blend.

fillable tank
COOKING TIME: 5 minutes

Fill the water tank with water.

Place the berries, date, and chia seeds in the blending bowl.

Set the steam timer for 5 minutes. When the timer goes off, blend the berries, date, and chia seeds with the cooking liquid.

stovetop
COOKING TIME: 4 minutes

In a 2-quart saucepan set over high heat, bring ½ cup water to a boil, about 2 minutes. Add the berries, date, and chia seeds; reduce the heat to medium-low; and place a tight-fitting lid on the saucepan. Steam for 2 minutes.

Transfer the berries, date, and chia seeds to a blender (or food processor) with the remaining cooking liquid and blend until combined.

NOTE: After it has cooled and thickened in the refrigerator, this puree makes a great and filling afternoon snack for a toddler or adult. Its texture is like a pudding, and to make it into more of a pudding, stir an additional 2 teaspoons chia seeds into the warm puree before putting in the refrigerator. This puree is also a great faux jam; just serve it on your morning toast as a delicious spread.

STORAGE INFORMATION
3 days refrigerator
2 months freezer

banana, oat, sweet potato, and allspice puree

½ medium banana, peeled and cut into 1-inch pieces

1 cup peeled and cubed sweet potato

2 tablespoons quick-cooking oats

¼ teaspoon ground allspice

This subtly sweet puree is nice and gentle on baby's tummy. It can be served either warm or cold.

water level
COOKING TIME: 25 minutes

Pour water into the tank to the highest level (mine is level 3, which equals about 1 cup water).

Put the banana, sweet potato, oats, and allspice in the steamer basket or cooking compartment.

Start the cooking process. When the cooking process is done, pour the contents of the steamer basket into the blending bowl with the cooking liquid. Blend.

fillable tank
COOKING TIME: 20 minutes

Fill the water tank with water.

Place the banana, sweet potato, oats, and allspice in the blending bowl.

Set the steam timer for 20 minutes. When the timer goes off, blend all the ingredients with the cooking liquid.

stovetop
COOKING TIME: 12 minutes

In a 2-quart saucepan set over high heat, bring ⅔ cup water to a boil, about 2 minutes. Add the banana, sweet potato, oats, and allspice; reduce the heat to medium-low; and place a tight-fitting lid on the saucepan. Steam for about 10 minutes, or until the sweet potato cubes are tender when pierced with a fork.

Transfer the contents of the saucepan to a blender (or food processor) with the remaining cooking liquid and blend. If the puree is too thick, add a few teaspoons of water and blend until smooth.

NOTE: Instead of dry oats, you could add a different grain—just make sure it's cooked. For example, use cooked quinoa or brown rice in place of dry oats.

STORAGE INFORMATION
3 days refrigerator
2 months freezer

beet, squash, and yogurt puree

1 small beet, peeled and cut into small cubes (about ½ cup)

1 cup peeled, seeded, and cubed butternut squash

½ cup plain full-fat Greek yogurt

Beets have a sweet, earthy flavor that is balanced perfectly when combined with squash. If you don't have squash on hand, I'd recommend using an equal amount of sweet potato or apple. I like using Greek yogurt for protein in this recipe, although you can substitute full-fat coconut milk.

water level

COOKING TIME: 25 minutes

Pour water into the tank to the highest level (mine is level 3, which equals about 1 cup water).

Put the beet and squash in the steamer basket or cooking compartment.

Start the cooking process. When the cooking process is done, drain and discard a little of the cooking liquid (or all of it for a thicker puree). Pour the beet and squash into the blending bowl, add the yogurt, and blend.

fillable tank

COOKING TIME: 25 minutes

Fill the water tank with water.

Place the beet and squash in the blending bowl.

Set the steam timer for 25 minutes. When the timer goes off, drain and discard a little of the cooking liquid (or all of it for a thicker puree). Add the yogurt to the blending bowl and blend.

stovetop

COOKING TIME: 13 minutes

In a 2-quart saucepan set over high heat, bring 1 cup water to a boil, about 3 minutes. Add the beet and squash, reduce the heat to medium-low, and place a tight-fitting lid on the saucepan. Steam for about 10 minutes, or until the beet cubes are easily pierced with a fork. Drain and discard a little of the cooking liquid off (or all of it for a thicker puree).

Transfer the beet and squash to a blender (or food processor) with the remaining cooking liquid, add the yogurt, and blend.

NOTE: This puree tastes great with a dash of ground cinnamon, nutmeg, or allspice added along with the yogurt before blending.

STORAGE INFORMATION
3 days refrigerator
2 months freezer

peach, plum, pepper, and grain puree

1 medium peach, pitted and cut into large pieces (about 1 cup)

1 medium plum, pitted and cut into large pieces (about 1 cup)

¼ medium bell pepper, ribs removed, seeded, and cut into strips (about ¼ cup)

¼ cup cooked brown rice

The bold sweetness of these stone fruits—peaches and plums—combines perfectly with mild bell peppers and grains to keep baby nourished. I like using red bell peppers in this puree, because when steamed, they become slightly sweet. If your baby isn't a big fan of bell peppers but you still want them to try them, this is the puree to make.

water level
COOKING TIME: 25 minutes

Pour water into the tank to the highest level (mine is level 3, which equals about 1 cup water).

Put the peach, plum, and bell pepper in the steamer basket or cooking compartment.

Start the cooking process. When the cooking process is done, drain and discard a little of the cooking liquid (or all of it for a thicker puree). Pour the peach, plum, and bell pepper into the blending bowl with the remaining cooking liquid, add the cooked brown rice, and blend.

fillable tank
COOKING TIME: 20 minutes

Fill the water tank with water.

Place the peach, plum, and bell pepper in the blending bowl.

Set the steam timer for 20 minutes. When the timer goes off, drain and discard a little of the cooking liquid (or all of it for a thicker puree). Add the cooked brown rice to the blending bowl and blend.

stovetop
COOKING TIME: 11 minutes

In a 2-quart saucepan set over high heat, bring 1 cup water to a boil, about 3 minutes. Add the peach, plum, and bell pepper; reduce the heat to medium-low; and place a tight-fitting lid on the saucepan. Steam for about 8 minutes, or until the bell pepper strips are easily pierced with a fork. Drain and discard a little of the cooking liquid (or all of it for a thicker puree).

Transfer the peach, plum, and bell pepper to a blender (or food processor) with the remaining cooking liquid, add the cooked brown rice, and blend.

NOTES: Instead of brown rice, you can use another cooked grain, like quinoa or barley.

This puree is delicious with a pinch of a savory fresh or dried herb, like thyme, oregano, or rosemary, that is added before blending.

STORAGE INFORMATION
3 days refrigerator
2 months freezer

eggplant, berry, and grain puree

½ cup (1-inch cubes) peeled eggplant

1 cup berries
¼ cup cooked grain

Eggplant is not typically found in commercially prepared baby food, but it's an ingredient I love, so I added some to a berry puree, and lo and behold, my son loved it. Eggplant by itself can be a little bitter, so in this puree it's mixed with sweet berries; I like to use strawberries, hulled and cut into pieces. When you're first introducing eggplant, be sure to peel off the purple skin. I like using quinoa in this recipe for the additional protein it provides.

water level
COOKING TIME: 25 minutes

Pour water into the tank to the highest level (mine is level 3, which equals about 1 cup water).

Put the eggplant and berries in the steamer basket or cooking compartment.

Start the cooking process. When the cooking process is done, pour the eggplant and berries into the blending bowl with the cooking liquid. Add the cooked grain and blend.

fillable tank
COOKING TIME: 20 minutes

Fill the water tank with water.

Place the eggplant and berries into the blending bowl.

Set the steam timer for 20 minutes. When the timer goes off, add the cooked grain to the blending bowl and blend.

stovetop
COOKING TIME: 8 minutes

In a 2-quart saucepan set over high heat, bring 1 cup water to a boil, about 3 minutes. Add the eggplant and berries, reduce the heat to medium-low, and place a tight-fitting lid on the saucepan. Steam for about 5 minutes, or until the eggplant pieces are easily pierced with a fork.

Transfer the eggplant and berries to a blender (or food processor) with the remaining cooking liquid, add the cooked grain, and blend.

STORAGE INFORMATION
3 days refrigerator
2 months freezer

berry, quinoa, and yogurt puree

1½ cups strawberries, raspberries, blueberries, blackberries, or a combination

¼ cup cooked quinoa

¼ cup plain full-fat Greek yogurt

Berries, berries, berries! As soon as my son tried berries—blueberries and raspberries specifically—he loved them and anything containing them. In the winter I simply use frozen organic berries in place of fresh ones, so that he can enjoy their nutritional benefits and this protein-filled breakfast all year-round.

water level
COOKING TIME: 10 minutes

Pour water into the tank to the lowest level (mine is level 1, which equals about ⅓ cup water).

Put the berries in the steamer basket or cooking compartment.

Start the cooking process. When the cooking process is done, pour the berries into the blending bowl with the cooking liquid. Add the quinoa and yogurt and blend.

fillable tank
COOKING TIME: 5 minutes

Fill the water tank with water.

Place the berries in the blending bowl.

Set the steam timer for 5 minutes. When the timer goes off, add the quinoa and yogurt and blend.

stovetop
COOKING TIME: 4 minutes

In a 2-quart saucepan set over high heat, bring ½ cup water to a boil, about 2 minutes. Add the berries, reduce the heat to medium-low, and place a tight-fitting lid on the saucepan. Steam for 2 minutes.

Transfer the berries to a blender (or food processor) with the remaining cooking liquid, add the quinoa and yogurt, and blend.

NOTE: Instead of quinoa, you can add another cooked grain, like oatmeal or brown rice.

STORAGE INFORMATION
3 days refrigerator
2 months freezer

beef, avocado, and black bean puree

1 ounce ground beef, crumbled into chunks

½ Hass avocado, pit and peel removed, cut into pieces

¼ cup cooked black beans, rinsed and drained

This iron- and protein-filled puree is really nice and palatable for baby because the smooth texture of black beans and avocado envelop the beef.

water level
COOKING TIME: 25 minutes

Pour water into the tank to the highest level (mine is level 3, which equals about 1 cup water).

Place the beef, avocado, and beans in the steamer basket or cooking compartment.

Start the cooking process. When the cooking process is done, pour the contents of the steamer basket into the blending bowl with the cooking liquid. Blend.

fillable tank
COOKING TIME: 20 minutes

Fill the water tank with water.

Place the beef, avocado, and beans in the blending bowl.

Set the steam timer for 20 minutes. When the timer goes off, blend the contents of the blending bowl with the cooking liquid.

stovetop
COOKING TIME: 13 minutes

In a 2-quart saucepan set over high heat, bring 1 cup water to a boil, about 3 minutes. Add the beef, avocado, and beans; reduce the heat to medium-low; and place a tight-fitting lid on the saucepan. Steam for about 10 minutes, or until the beef chunks are cooked through and no pink remains in the center.

Transfer the contents of the saucepan to a blender (or food processor) with the cooking liquid and blend.

NOTES: This puree is great with the addition of dried or chopped fresh herbs like oregano, rosemary, parsley, or basil, or ground spices like cumin or allspice; add your choice before blending.

If the puree seems a little too thick, add a few teaspoons of water until the desired consistency is reached.

STORAGE INFORMATION
2 days refrigerator
do not freeze

chicken, squash, and potato puree

1 to 2 ounces skinless, boneless chicken breast, cut into ½- to 1-inch cubes

½ cup peeled, seeded, and cubed butternut squash

1 small red or yellow potato, peeled and cut into ½- to 1-inch cubes (about ¼ cup)

1 teaspoon extra-virgin olive oil

Chicken is a great source of lean protein for your baby. When combined with squash and potatoes, this puree is thick and creamy. I like adding a teaspoon of olive oil before blending this puree for some healthy fats and to make it silky smooth.

water level
COOKING TIME: 25 minutes

Pour water into the tank to the highest level (mine is level 3, which equals about 1 cup water).

Place the chicken, squash, and potato in the steamer basket or cooking compartment.

Start the cooking process. When the cooking process is done, pour the contents of the steamer basket into the blending bowl with the cooking liquid, add the olive oil, and blend.

fillable tank
COOKING TIME: 25 minutes

Fill the water tank with water.

Place the chicken, squash, and potato in the blending bowl.

Set the steam timer for 25 minutes. When the timer goes off, add the olive oil to the blending bowl and blend.

stovetop
COOKING TIME: 13 minutes

In a 2-quart saucepan set over high heat, bring 1 cup water to a boil, about 3 minutes. Add the chicken, squash, and potato; reduce the heat to medium-low; and place a tight-fitting lid on the saucepan. Steam for about 10 minutes, or until the chicken cubes are cooked through (there should be no pink remaining in the center when you cut into a piece, or use a meat thermometer to make sure the internal temperature of the chicken has reached 165°F).

Transfer the contents of the saucepan to a blender (or food processor) with the cooking liquid, add the olive oil, and blend.

NOTE: This puree is great with a pinch of ground cinnamon, nutmeg, or allspice blended in with the olive oil.

STORAGE INFORMATION
2 days refrigerator
2 months freezer

chicken, kale, and quinoa puree

2 ounces skinless, boneless chicken breast, cut into ½- to ¾-inch cubes

1 cup stemmed and chopped kale

¼ cup cooked quinoa

I like telling my baby what he is eating when I am feeding it to him: "This is chicken, kale, and quinoa." I want him to appreciate all sorts of flavors when he is older, and I always feel as if he is eating a fancy little salad in the form of a puree when I feed him this one.

water level
COOKING TIME: 25 minutes

Pour water into the tank to the highest level (mine is level 3, which equals about 1 cup water).

Put the chicken and kale in the steamer basket or cooking compartment.

Start the cooking process. When the cooking process is done, pour the chicken and kale into the blending bowl with the cooking liquid. Add the quinoa and blend.

fillable tank
COOKING TIME: 20 minutes

Fill the water tank with water.

Place the chicken and kale in the blending bowl.

Set the steam timer for 20 minutes. When the timer goes off, add the quinoa to the blending bowl and blend.

stovetop
COOKING TIME: 11 minutes

In a 2-quart saucepan set over high heat, bring 1 cup water to a boil, about 3 minutes. Add the chicken and kale, reduce the heat to medium-low, and place a tight-fitting lid on the saucepan. Steam for about 8 minutes, or until the chicken cubes are cooked through (there should be no pink remaining in the center when you cut into a piece, or use a meat thermometer to make sure the internal temperature of the chicken has reached 165°F).

Transfer the chicken and kale to a blender (or food processor) with the remaining cooking liquid, add the cooked quinoa, and blend.

NOTE: Stir in a teaspoon of extra-virgin olive oil and some dried or chopped fresh basil or parsley after this puree is done cooking to take it to the next level.

STORAGE INFORMATION
2 days refrigerator
2 months freezer

chicken, pea, and pear puree

2 ounces skinless, boneless chicken breast, cut into ½- to ¾-inch cubes

½ cup fresh or frozen peas

1 pear, cored and cut into pieces (about 1 cup; skin on is okay)

You'll discover the perfect combination of sweet and savory in this puree. It's also a great combination of lean protein, vegetable, and fruits, and because of the peas, it has a really nice gentle green color.

water level

COOKING TIME: 25 minutes

Pour water into the tank to the highest level (mine is level 3, which equals about 1 cup water).

Put the chicken, peas, and pear in the steamer basket or cooking compartment.

Start the cooking process. When the cooking process is done, pour the chicken, peas, and pear into the blending bowl with the cooking liquid. Blend.

fillable tank

COOKING TIME: 20 minutes

Fill the water tank with water.

Place the chicken, peas, and pear in the blending bowl.

Set the steam timer for 20 minutes. When the timer goes off, blend the chicken, peas, and pear with the cooking liquid.

stovetop

COOKING TIME: 11 minutes

In a 2-quart saucepan set over high heat, bring 1 cup water to a boil, about 3 minutes. Add the chicken, peas, and pear; reduce the heat to medium-low; and place a tight-fitting lid on the saucepan. Steam for about 8 minutes, or until the chicken cubes are cooked through (there should be no pink remaining in the center when you cut into a piece, or use a meat thermometer to make sure the internal temperature of the chicken has reached 165°F).

Transfer the chicken, peas, and pear to a blender (or food processor) with the remaining cooking liquid and blend.

NOTE: Stir in a teaspoon of extra-virgin olive oil and some ground cinnamon or chopped fresh basil or parsley after the puree is done cooking.

STORAGE INFORMATION
2 days refrigerator
2 months freezer

pork, sweet potato, and apple puree

1 ounce pork, cut into ½- to ¾-inch cubes

½ cup peeled and cubed sweet potato

1 medium apple, cored and cut into cubes (about 1 cup; skin on is okay)

Pork is so delicious that every time I eat it I wonder why I don't have it more often! Mixed with sweet potatoes and apples, it makes a delicious, slightly sweet puree. I recommend a pork chop or tenderloin for this.

water level
COOKING TIME: 25 minutes

Pour water into the tank to the highest level (mine is level 3, which equals about 1 cup water).

Put the pork, sweet potato, and apple in the steamer basket or cooking compartment.

Start the cooking process. When the cooking process is done, pour the pork, sweet potato, and apple into the blending bowl with the cooking liquid. Blend.

fillable tank
COOKING TIME: 20 minutes

Fill the water tank with water.

Place the pork, sweet potato, and apple in the blending bowl.

Set the steam timer for 20 minutes. When the timer goes off, blend the pork, sweet potato, and apple with the cooking liquid.

stovetop
COOKING TIME: 13 minutes

In a 2-quart saucepan set over high heat, bring 1 cup water to a boil, about 3 minutes. Add the pork, sweet potato, and apple; reduce the heat to medium-low; and place a tight-fitting lid on the saucepan. Steam for about 10 minutes, or until the pork is cooked through (there should be no pink remaining in the center when you cut into a piece, or use a meat thermometer to make sure the internal temperature has reached 145°F) and the sweet potato and apple cubes are easily pierced with a fork.

Transfer the pork, sweet potato, and apple to a blender (or food processor) with the remaining cooking liquid and blend.

NOTE: Before blending, add a teaspoon of extra-virgin olive oil and some ground cinnamon, nutmeg, or allspice to this puree. If you're looking for a delicious pork and sweet potato recipe that uses the same ingredients in a meal for the rest of the family, I have a sheet pan supper recipe on my blog (sweetphi.com/extras).

STORAGE INFORMATION
2 days refrigerator
2 months freezer

salmon, sweet potato, and apple puree

1 ounce deboned salmon, cut into a few 1-inch pieces

½ cup peeled and cubed sweet potato

1 medium apple, peeled, cored, and cut into ½- to ¾-inch cubes (about 1 cup)

1 teaspoon extra-virgin olive oil

⅓ cup no-sodium chicken or vegetable broth (optional)

This puree is a great way to introduce salmon into your baby's diet. I like to add a dash of olive oil before blending, as it makes the puree silky smooth.

water level
COOKING TIME: 25 minutes

Pour water into the tank to the highest level (mine is level 3, which equals about 1 cup water).

Place the salmon, sweet potato, and apple in the steamer basket or cooking compartment.

Start the cooking process. When the cooking process is done, remove the salmon from the steamer basket and take off and discard the skin. Place the skinless salmon in the blending bowl and pour in the remaining contents of the steamer basket. Drizzle the olive oil on top and blend. Alternatively, drain and discard the cooking liquid before adding the contents of the steamer basket to the blending bowl. Add the skinless salmon, drizzle it with olive oil, and add the broth before blending, a tablespoon at a time, until the desired consistency is reached.

fillable tank
COOKING TIME: 20 minutes

Fill the water tank with water.

Place the salmon, sweet potato, and apple in the blending bowl.

Set the steam timer for 20 minutes. When the timer goes off, remove the salmon from the blending bowl and take off and discard the skin. Return the salmon to the blending bowl, drizzle the olive oil on top, and blend. Alternatively, drain and discard the cooking liquid before returning the skinless salmon to the blending bowl and drizzling it with olive oil. Add the broth and blend.

stovetop
COOKING TIME: 15 minutes

In a 2-quart saucepan set over high heat, bring 1 cup water to a boil, about 3 minutes. Add the salmon, sweet potato, and apple; reduce the heat to medium-low;

and place a tight-fitting lid on the saucepan. Steam for about 12 minutes, or until the salmon is cooked through (it shouldn't appear translucent when you break into a piece) and the sweet potato cubes are tender when pierced with a fork.

When the ingredients are done cooking, remove the salmon and take off and discard the skin. Transfer the salmon, apple, and sweet potato to a blender (or food processor) with the cooking liquid, add the olive oil, and blend. Alternatively, drain and discard the cooking liquid before transferring the skinless salmon, apple, and sweet potato to the blender. Add the broth, a tablespoon at a time, along with the olive oil and blend until the desired consistency is reached.

STORAGE INFORMATION
2 days refrigerator
2 months freezer

NOTE: Just a ¼ teaspoon (or less) of dried or chopped fresh basil, dill, or thyme all taste really good in this puree; add before blending.

fish, garlic, and cauliflower puree

1½ cups cauliflower florets

1 ounce skinned and deboned white fish, cut into a few 1-inch pieces

1 garlic clove, pressed

1 teaspoon extra-virgin olive oil

¼ cup no-sodium chicken or vegetable broth (optional)

When serving fish to your little one, make sure you're pairing it with ingredients that don't overpower it. I like to use varieties of white fish that are mild in taste, like halibut, cod, or snapper. For a milder taste and cleaner blend, use broth instead of the cooking liquid.

water level

COOKING TIME: 25 minutes

Pour water into the tank to the highest level (mine is level 3, which equals about 1 cup water).

Place the cauliflower, fish, and garlic in the steamer basket or cooking compartment.

Start the cooking process. When the cooking process is done, pour the contents of the steamer basket into the blending bowl with the cooking liquid. Add the olive oil and blend. Alternatively, drain and discard the cooking liquid before pouring the cauliflower, fish, and garlic into the blending bowl. Add the broth along with the olive oil and blend until the desired consistency is reached.

fillable tank

COOKING TIME: 20 minutes

Fill the water tank with water.

Place the cauliflower, fish, and garlic in the blending bowl.

Set the steam timer for 20 minutes. When the timer goes off, add the olive oil to the blending bowl and blend. Alternatively, you can drain and discard the cooking liquid and add the broth along with the olive oil before blending to the desired consistency.

stovetop

COOKING TIME: 13 minutes

In a 2-quart saucepan set over high heat, bring 1 cup water to a boil, about 3 minutes. Add the cauliflower, fish, and garlic; reduce the heat to medium-low; and place a tight-fitting lid on the saucepan. Steam for about 10 minutes, or until the cauliflower florets are tender when pierced with a fork.

Transfer the contents of the saucepan to a blender (or food processor) with the remaining cooking liquid, add the olive oil, and blend. Alternatively, you can drain and discard the cooking liquid before transferring the contents to the blender. Add the broth along with the olive oil and blend until the desired consistency is reached.

STORAGE INFORMATION
2 days refrigerator
2 months freezer

tofu, carrot, and cauliflower puree

2 ounces firm or extra-firm tofu, cut into ½- to ¾-inch cubes and drained (about 1 cup)

½ cup peeled and diced carrots

½ cup cauliflower florets

1 teaspoon extra-virgin olive oil

¼ teaspoon sweet paprika

In this velvety puree, tofu, carrot, and cauliflower are combined with a hint of paprika, which adds a smoky note. Sometimes I like adding a pinch of chili powder to this as well.

water level

COOKING TIME: 25 minutes

Pour water into the tank to the highest level (mine is level 3, which equals about 1 cup water).

Put the tofu, carrot, and cauliflower in the steamer basket or cooking compartment.

Start the cooking process. When the cooking process is done, drain and discard the cooking liquid. Pour the tofu, carrot, and cauliflower into the blending bowl and add the olive oil and paprika. Blend.

fillable tank

COOKING TIME: 20 minutes

Fill the water tank with water.

Place the tofu, carrot, and cauliflower in the blending bowl.

Set the steam timer for 20 minutes. When the timer goes off, drain and discard the cooking liquid. Add the olive oil and paprika to the blending bowl and blend until smooth.

stovetop

COOKING TIME: 13 minutes

In a 2-quart saucepan set over high heat, bring 1 cup water to a boil, about 3 minutes. Add the tofu, carrot, and cauliflower; reduce the heat to medium-low; and place a tight-fitting lid on the saucepan. Steam for about 10 minutes, or until the carrot and cauliflower pieces are easily pierced with a fork. Drain and discard the cooking liquid.

Transfer the tofu, carrot, and cauliflower to a blender (or food processor), add the olive oil and paprika, and blend.

STORAGE INFORMATION
3 days refrigerator
2 months freezer

tofu, squash, and green bean puree

2 ounces firm or extra-firm tofu, cut into ½- to ¾-inch cubes and drained (about 1 cup)

½ cup peeled, seeded, and cubed winter squash

½ cup (1-inch pieces) fresh or frozen trimmed green beans (about 3 ounces)

1 teaspoon extra-virgin olive oil

¼ teaspoon dried parsley

Tofu is super mild in taste and takes on the flavors of what it is cooked with or the spices added to it while cooking. Even if you don't like tofu, don't discount it for your little one; tofu is a fantastic source of plant-based protein and blends super silky smooth!

water level
COOKING TIME: 25 minutes

Pour water into the tank to the highest level (mine is level 3, which equals about 1 cup water).

Put the tofu, squash, and green beans in the steamer basket or cooking compartment.

Start the cooking process. When the cooking process is done, drain and discard the cooking liquid (if desired). Pour the tofu, squash, and green beans into the blending bowl and add the olive oil and parsley. Blend.

fillable tank
COOKING TIME: 25 minutes

Fill the water tank with water.

Place the tofu, squash, and green beans in the blending bowl.

Set the steam timer for 25 minutes. When the timer goes off, drain and discard the cooking liquid. Add the olive oil and parsley to the blending bowl and blend.

stovetop
COOKING TIME: 13 minutes

In a 2-quart saucepan set over high heat, bring 1 cup water to a boil, about 3 minutes. Add the tofu, squash, and green beans; reduce the heat to medium-low; and place a tight-fitting lid on the saucepan. Steam for about 10 minutes, or until the green beans and squash cubes are easily pierced with a fork. Drain and discard the cooking liquid.

Transfer the tofu, squash, and green beans to a blender (or food processor), add the olive oil and parsley, and blend.

STORAGE INFORMATION
3 days refrigerator
2 months freezer

tofu, sweet potato, and turmeric puree

2 ounces firm or extra-firm tofu, cut into ½- to ¾-inch cubes and drained (about 1 cup)

1 cup peeled and cubed sweet potato

1 teaspoon extra-virgin olive oil

¼ teaspoon ground turmeric

I love adding different spices to tofu, because it takes on the flavor of whatever it's cooked and seasoned with. Tofu, sweet potatoes, and turmeric blend together to form a mild and slightly sweet, bright yellow puree.

water level
COOKING TIME: 25 minutes

Pour water into the tank to the highest level (mine is level 3, which equals about 1 cup water).

Put the tofu and sweet potato in the steamer basket or cooking compartment.

Start the cooking process. When the cooking process is done, drain and discard the cooking liquid. Pour the tofu and sweet potato into the blending bowl and add the olive oil and turmeric. Blend.

fillable tank
COOKING TIME: 20 minutes

Fill the water tank with water.

Place the tofu and sweet potato in the blending bowl.

Set the steam timer for 20 minutes. When the timer goes off, drain and discard the cooking liquid. Add the olive oil and turmeric to the blending bowl and blend until smooth.

stovetop
COOKING TIME: 13 minutes

In a 2-quart saucepan set over high heat, bring 1 cup water to a boil, about 3 minutes. Add the tofu and sweet potato, reduce the heat to medium-low, and place a tight-fitting lid on the saucepan. Steam for about 10 minutes, or until the sweet potato cubes are easily pierced with a fork. Drain and discard the cooking liquid.

Transfer the tofu and sweet potato to a blender (or food processor), add the olive oil and turmeric, and blend.

STORAGE INFORMATION
3 days refrigerator
2 months freezer

lentil, pepper, and sweet potato puree

¼ bell pepper, seeded, ribs removed, and cut into strips (about ¼ cup)

1 cup peeled and cubed sweet potato

⅓ cup cooked red lentils

¼ cup no-sodium vegetable broth

1 teaspoon extra-virgin olive oil

¼ teaspoon chili powder

I love making red lentil stew in the winter. I've also turned it into a puree so my baby can enjoy it with me as he learns to explore and appreciate different spices, textures, and flavors. I like using red lentils because they cook quickly and break down almost completely for soups, but feel free to use any type of lentils here; just make sure they're cooked through, nice and soft.

water level

COOKING TIME: 25 minutes

Pour water into the tank to the highest level (mine is level 3, which equals about 1 cup water).

Put the bell pepper and sweet potato in the steamer basket or cooking compartment.

Start the cooking process. When the cooking process is done, drain and discard the cooking liquid. Pour the bell pepper and sweet potato into the blending bowl, add the cooked lentils, broth, olive oil, and chili powder. Blend.

fillable tank

COOKING TIME: 20 minutes

Fill the water tank with water.

Place the bell pepper and sweet potato in the blending bowl.

Set the steam timer for 20 minutes. When the timer goes off, drain and discard the cooking liquid. Add the cooked lentils, broth, olive oil, and chili powder to the blending bowl and blend.

stovetop

COOKING TIME: 13 minutes

In a 2-quart saucepan set over high heat, bring 1 cup water to a boil, about 3 minutes. Add the bell pepper and sweet potato, reduce the heat to medium-low, and place a tight-fitting lid on the saucepan. Steam for about 10 minutes, or until the sweet potato cubes are easily pierced with a fork. Drain and discard the cooking liquid.

Transfer the bell pepper and sweet potato to a blender (or food processor) and add the cooked lentils, broth, olive oil, and chili powder. Blend.

STORAGE INFORMATION
3 days refrigerator
2 months freezer

banana, mango, pear, and coconut milk puree

1 medium banana, peeled and cut into chunks

1 cup peeled, pitted, and cubed mango

1 medium pear, peeled, cored, and cut into pieces (about 1 cup)

¼ cup full-fat coconut milk

I love adding coconut milk to the purees I make for my baby because it is such a good source of plant-based saturated fat for his diet. In this recipe, there's a bright, sweet flavor from all the fruit. If you add a dash of ground cinnamon during the final blending, it ends up tasting almost like a tropical rice pudding. This also makes a good smoothie. Simply make the puree as is and freeze it into cubes; when you're ready to enjoy the smoothie, blend the cubes with 1¾ to 2 cups liquid (I like using unflavored almond milk). This makes two smoothies.

water level
COOKING TIME: 10 minutes

Pour water into the tank to the lowest level (mine is level 1, which equals about ⅓ cup water).

Put the banana, mango, and pear in the steamer basket or cooking compartment.

Start the cooking process. When the cooking process is done, drain and discard the cooking liquid. Pour the banana, mango, and pear into the blending bowl, add the coconut milk, and blend.

fillable tank
COOKING TIME: 5 minutes

Fill the water tank with water.

Place the banana, mango, and pear in the blending bowl.

Set the steam timer for 5 minutes. When the timer goes off, drain and discard the cooking liquid. Add the coconut milk and blend.

stovetop
COOKING TIME: 4 minutes

In a 2-quart saucepan set over high heat, bring ½ cup water to a boil, about 2 minutes. Add the banana, mango, and pear; reduce the heat to medium-low; and place a tight-fitting lid on the saucepan. Steam for 2 minutes. Drain and discard the cooking liquid.

Transfer the banana, mango, and pear to a blender (or food processor), pour in the coconut milk, and blend.

STORAGE INFORMATION
3 days refrigerator
2 months freezer

mango, banana, cauliflower, and spinach puree

1 cup peeled, pitted, and cubed fresh or frozen mango

½ medium banana, peeled and sliced (about ½ cup)

½ cup cauliflower florets

½ cup baby spinach

Confession time: I threw this puree together when I had some random ingredients in my fridge that I needed to use. They ended up turning into one of the most delicious purees I've tried, and my son loved it! This also makes a delicious smoothie. Simply make the puree as is and freeze it into cubes; when you're ready to enjoy the smoothie, blend the cubes with 1¾ to 2 cups liquid (I like using unflavored almond milk). This makes two smoothies.

water level
COOKING TIME: 17 minutes

Pour water into the tank to the medium level (mine is level 2, which equals about ⅔ cup water).

Put the mango, banana, cauliflower, and spinach in the steamer basket or cooking compartment.

Start the cooking process. When the cooking process is done, drain and discard a little of the cooking liquid (or all of it for a thicker puree). Pour the contents of the steamer basket into the blending bowl. Blend.

fillable tank
COOKING TIME: 10 minutes

Fill the water tank with water.

Place the mango, banana, cauliflower, and spinach in the blending bowl.

Set the steam timer for 10 minutes. When the timer goes off, drain and discard a little of the cooking liquid (or all of it for a thicker puree). Blend the contents of the blending bowl with the remaining cooking liquid.

stovetop
COOKING TIME: 4 minutes

In a 2-quart saucepan set over high heat, bring ½ cup water to a boil, about 2 minutes. Add the mango, banana, cauliflower, and spinach; reduce the heat to medium-low; and place a tight-fitting lid on the saucepan. Steam for 2 minutes. Drain and discard a little of the cooking liquid (or all of it for a thicker puree).

Transfer the contents of the saucepan to a blender (or food processor) with the remaining cooking liquid and blend until smooth.

STORAGE INFORMATION
3 days refrigerator
2 months freezer

pineapple, sweet potato, and ginger puree

1 cup peeled, cored, and cubed pineapple

1 cup peeled and cubed sweet potato

¼ teaspoon grated fresh ginger

Pineapple is super sweet, but here it's toned down a bit by combining it with sweet potatoes and a touch of fresh ginger. This sweet puree is a tropical treat in the summertime and is easily made into ice pops (see Note).

water level
COOKING TIME: 25 minutes

Pour water into the tank to the highest level (mine is level 3, which equals about 1 cup of water).

Put the pineapple and sweet potato in the steamer basket or cooking compartment.

Start the cooking process. When the cooking process is done, drain and discard some of the cooking liquid, reserving 2 to 4 tablespoons. Pour the pineapple and sweet potato into the blending bowl with 2 tablespoons of the reserved cooking liquid, adding more as needed to reach the desired consistency. Add the ginger and blend.

fillable tank
COOKING TIME: 20 minutes

Fill the water tank with water.

Place the pineapple and sweet potato in the blending bowl.

Set the steam timer for 20 minutes. When the timer goes off, drain and discard a little of the cooking liquid, reserving 2 to 4 tablespoons. Add the ginger to the blending bowl with 2 tablespoons of the reserved cooking liquid and blend, adding more as needed to reach the desired consistency.

stovetop
COOKING TIME: 13 minutes

In a 2-quart saucepan set over high heat, bring 1 cup water to a boil, about 3 minutes. Add the pineapple and sweet potato, reduce the heat to medium-low, and place a tight-fitting lid on the saucepan. Steam for about 10 minutes, or until the sweet potato cubes are easily pierced with a fork. Drain and discard a little of the cooking liquid, reserving 2 to 4 tablespoons.

Transfer the pineapple and sweet potato to a blender (or food processor) with 2 tablespoons of the remaining cooking liquid, add the ginger, and blend, adding more cooking liquid as needed to reach the desired consistency.

NOTE: To make ice pops, prepare the puree as directed but do not drain any cooking liquid before blending. Pour the puree into an ice pop mold and freeze until solid, about 3 hours. To serve, run the mold under warm water for a few seconds; the ice pops should come right out. As a general rule, 1 cup puree yields 2 to 2½ ice pops, so using this recipe, I usually get 4 or 5.

STORAGE INFORMATION
3 days refrigerator
2 months freezer

berry, avocado, and coconut milk puree

1½ cups strawberries, raspberries, blueberries, blackberries, or a combination

½ Hass avocado, pitted and skin removed

¼ cup full-fat coconut milk

This puree is wonderful for baby, but it's also great for your own morning smoothie! Simply make the puree as is and freeze it into cubes; when you're ready to enjoy the smoothie, blend the cubes with 1¾ to 2 cups liquid (I like using unflavored almond milk). This makes two smoothies. As soon as my son could drink out of sippy cups, I put a little of my morning smoothie in his cup!

water level

COOKING TIME: 10 minutes

Pour water into the tank to the lowest level (mine is level 1, which equals about ⅓ cup water).

Put the berries and avocado in the steamer basket or cooking compartment.

Start the cooking process. When the cooking process is done, drain and discard the cooking liquid. Pour the berries and avocado into the blending bowl, add the coconut milk, and blend.

fillable tank

COOKING TIME: 5 minutes

Fill the water tank with water.

Place the berries and avocado in the blending bowl.

Set the steam timer for 5 minutes. When the timer goes off, drain and discard the cooking liquid. Add the coconut milk to the blending bowl and blend.

stovetop

COOKING TIME: 4 minutes

In a 2-quart saucepan set over high heat, bring ½ cup water to a boil, about 2 minutes. Add the berries and avocado, reduce the heat to medium-low, and place a tight-fitting lid on the saucepan. Steam for 2 minutes. Drain and discard the cooking liquid.

Transfer the berries and avocado to a blender (or food processor), pour in the coconut milk, and blend.

STORAGE INFORMATION
3 days refrigerator
2 months freezer

beet, apple, and watermelon puree

1 medium apple, peeled, cored, and cut into ½- to ¾-inch cubes (about 1 cup)

1 cup cubed seedless watermelon

¼ cup peeled and cubed beets

The sweetness of the apple and watermelon in this recipe covers up any earthy beet flavors. Purple beets add a really pretty color to this puree, but orange or white beets also work if you don't want to stain your hands red! This recipe works as a puree or as an ice pop (see Note).

water level
COOKING TIME: 25 minutes

Pour water into the tank to the highest level (mine is level 3, which equals about 1 cup water).

Put the apple, watermelon, and beet in the steamer basket or cooking compartment.

Start the cooking process. When the cooking process is done, drain and discard a little of the cooking liquid (or all of it for a thicker puree). Pour the apple, watermelon, and beet into the blending bowl with the remaining cooking liquid. Blend.

fillable tank
COOKING TIME: 20 minutes

Fill the water tank with water.

Place the apple, watermelon, and beet into the blending bowl.

Set the steam timer for 20 minutes. When the timer goes off, drain and discard a little of the cooking liquid (or all of it for a thicker puree). Blend the contents of the blending bowl with the remaining cooking liquid.

stovetop
COOKING TIME: 13 minutes

In a 2-quart saucepan set over high heat, bring 1 cup water to a boil, about 3 minutes. Add the apple, watermelon, and beet; reduce the heat to medium-low; and place a tight-fitting lid on the saucepan. Steam for about 10 minutes, or until the apple and beet cubes are easily pierced with a fork. Drain and discard a little of the cooking liquid (or all of it for a thicker puree).

Transfer the contents of the saucepan to a blender (or food processor) with the remaining cooking liquid and blend.

NOTE: To make ice pops, make the puree as directed but do not drain any cooking liquid before blending. After blending, pour the puree into an ice pop mold and freeze until solid, about 3 hours. To serve, run the mold under warm water for a few seconds; the ice pops should come right out. As a general rule, 1 cup puree yields 2 to 2½ ice pops, so using this recipe, I usually get 4 or 5.

STORAGE INFORMATION
3 days refrigerator
2 months freezer

peach, nectarine, and mango puree

1 medium peach, pitted and cut into ½- to ¾-inch cubes (about 1 cup)

½ medium nectarine, pitted and cut into ½- to ¾-inch cubes (about ½ cup)

¾ cup peeled, pitted, and cubed fresh or frozen mango

Sweet and tart, this peach, nectarine, and mango puree is a bright orange color and has just the right mix of summer flavors to make it perfect for an ice pop (see Note).

water level
COOKING TIME: 10 minutes

Pour water into the tank to the lowest level (mine is level 1, which equals about ⅓ cup water).

Put the peach, nectarine, and mango in the steamer basket or cooking compartment.

Start the cooking process. When the cooking process is done, pour the peach, nectarine, and mango into the blending bowl with the cooking liquid. Blend.

fillable tank
COOKING TIME: 5 minutes

Fill the water tank with water.

Place the peach, nectarine, and mango in the blending bowl.

Set the steam timer for 5 minutes. When the timer goes off, blend the peach, nectarine, and mango with the cooking liquid.

stovetop
COOKING TIME: 4 minutes

In a 2-quart saucepan set over high heat, bring ½ cup water to a boil, about 2 minutes. Add the peach, nectarine, and mango; reduce the heat to medium-low; and place a tight-fitting lid on the saucepan. Steam for 2 minutes.

Transfer the peach, nectarine, and mango to a blender (or food processor) with the cooking liquid and blend.

NOTE: To make ice pops, prepare the puree as directed, pour the blended puree into an ice pop mold, and freeze until solid, about 3 hours. To serve, run the mold under warm water for a few seconds; the ice pops should come right out. As a general rule, 1 cup of puree yields 2 to 2½ ice pops, so using this recipe, I usually get 4 or 5.

STORAGE INFORMATION
3 days refrigerator
2 months freezer

block four

starting solids

TYPICALLY 9 TO 12 MONTHS

Starting solids is all about serving soft foods that can be mashed with a fork or left chunkier for babies to pick up by themselves. However, any of the recipes in this chapter can also be made into purees.

During this stage of starting solids, babies begin to feed themselves and start picking up food on their own. This is such a fun (and sometimes messy) endeavor. You can now make baby meatballs (see pages 143 and 170) and add a whole range of new flavors and textures to wholesome meals made in the baby food maker.

In this chapter, recipes are made into purees with alternative serving suggestions, for example, draining the cooking liquid and making a thicker puree, or leaving it as solids to either mash with a fork or let baby pick up and eat on their own.

Baby Shrimp Scampi 139

Baby Barbecue Chicken and Sweet Potatoes 140

Baby Meatballs with Carrots and Herbs 143

Baby Bolognese 144

Beef and Broccoli with Grain 147

Broccoli "Rice" and Cheddar 148

Chicken, Broccoli, and Cheese 149

Tofu, Cauliflower, and Cheese 150

Chicken, Sweet Potatoes, and Cumin 152

White Fish Chowder 153

Ginger-Tomato Chicken and Sweet Potatoes 154

Secretly Carrot Cheddar Cheese Sauce 155

Cilantro Lime Cauliflower "Rice" 156

Teriyaki Salmon, Broccoli, and Brown Rice 158

Gentle Baby Chili 159

Herby Salmon and Potatoes 160

Ground Beef, Peas, and Potatoes 162

Indian-Spiced Sweet Potatoes and Carrots 163

Lemony Quinoa Chicken 164

Salmon, Apricot, and Sweet Potatoes 165

Lemony Zucchini, Asparagus, and Green Beans 167

Potato Leek Soup 168

Savory Apple-Turkey Meatballs 170

Slightly Balsamic Apple, Chicken, and Potatoes 171

Basil, Tomato, and Winter Squash Soup 173

Turmeric Potatoes and Chicken 174

Tuscan White Bean Soup 177

baby shrimp scampi

2 ounces shrimp, peeled, deveined, and tails removed

1 garlic clove, crushed

Juice of ¼ lemon (about 1 tablespoon)

2 tablespoons no-sodium chicken or vegetable broth

1 tablespoon unsalted butter

1 teaspoon extra-virgin olive oil

¼ teaspoon dried parsley

I love, love, love shrimp scampi. The buttery, lemony sauce is just irresistible, so I wanted to create a version for my son. Once he started eating more solids, I served this over whole-wheat orzo, pasta, and even on bread, like a shrimp toast. You can blend this more or less depending on where your child is with solids. I've made this into a puree, a thicker puree, and then a chunky one as he became more accustomed to solids.

water level
COOKING TIME: 25 minutes

Pour water into the tank to the highest level (mine is level 3, which equals about 1 cup water).

Place the shrimp and garlic in the steamer basket or cooking compartment. Drizzle the lemon juice on top of the shrimp.

Start the cooking process. When the cooking process is done, drain and discard the cooking liquid.

Pour the shrimp and garlic into the blending bowl. Add the broth, butter, olive oil, and parsley. Pulse a few times (for a chunkier food) or until the desired consistency is reached.

fillable tank
COOKING TIME: 20 minutes

Fill the water tank with water.

Place the shrimp and garlic in the blending bowl and sprinkle the lemon juice on top.

Set the steam timer for 20 minutes. When the timer goes off, drain and discard the cooking liquid, leaving the shrimp and garlic in the blending bowl.

Add the broth, butter, olive oil, and parsley. Pulse a few times (for a chunkier food) or until the desired consistency is reached.

stovetop
COOKING TIME: 11 minutes

In a 2-quart saucepan set over high heat, bring 1 cup water to a boil, about 3 minutes. Add the shrimp, garlic, and lemon juice; reduce the heat to medium-low; and place a tight-fitting lid on the saucepan. Steam for about 8 minutes, or until the shrimp is no longer translucent.

When the shrimp is done, drain the cooking liquid.

Transfer the shrimp and garlic to a blender (or food processor) and add the broth, butter, olive oil, and parsley. Pulse a few times (for a chunkier food) or until the desired consistency is reached.

NOTE: To prepare this as an adult dish, simply add ¼ teaspoon kosher salt and a pinch of crushed red pepper flakes, and do not puree it. I like serving this over whole-wheat pasta, orzo, or with some crusty bread. You can also make shrimp toast by piling the shrimp onto toasted rustic Italian bread.

STORAGE INFORMATION
3 days refrigerator
2 months freezer

baby barbecue chicken and sweet potatoes

BARBECUE SAUCE

1 tablespoon tomato paste

1 tablespoon pure maple syrup

¼ teaspoon chili powder

¼ teaspoon sweet paprika

CHICKEN AND SWEET POTATOES

2 ounces skinless, boneless chicken breast, cut into ½- to ¾-inch cubes

1 medium sweet potato, peeled and cut into ½- to ¾-inch cubes (about 1 cup)

When I realized store-bought barbecue sauce has several ingredients that are no-no's for babies (mainly honey or corn syrup and sugar in higher quantities per serving than they should have), I made a little bowl of "baby barbecue sauce" for my son. I had a friend over who was skeptical that it would still taste good without those ingredients. I'm happy to report that my friend not only loved it, but she started making baby barbecue sauce for her own family. Give it a try—you won't even miss the sugar!

Make the barbecue sauce: In a small bowl, whisk together all the ingredients for the barbecue sauce and set aside. The sauce can be made ahead of time and refrigerated in an airtight container for up to 1 week; warm it in the microwave for 20 seconds before using.

Cook the chicken and sweet potatoes according to your preferred method below.

water level

COOKING TIME: 25 minutes

Pour water into the tank to the highest level (mine is level 3, which equals about 1 cup water).

Place the chicken and sweet potato in the steamer basket or cooking compartment.

Start the cooking process. When the cooking process is done, remove the steamer basket and allow the chicken and sweet potato to cool for a few minutes. Transfer it to a serving bowl, pour on the barbecue sauce, stirring everything together if desired, and feed it to your little one.

fillable tank

COOKING TIME: 20 minutes

Fill the water tank with water.

Place the chicken and sweet potato in the blending bowl.

Set the steam timer for 20 minutes. When the timer goes off, carefully remove the chicken and sweet potato with tongs or a fork, draining any excess cooking liquid. Allow the chicken and

sweet potato to cool for a few minutes. Transfer it to a serving bowl, pour on the barbecue sauce, stirring everything together if desired, and feed it to your little one.

stovetop

COOKING TIME: 15 minutes

In a 2-quart saucepan set over high heat, bring 1 cup water to a boil, about 3 minutes. Add the chicken and sweet potato, reduce the heat to medium-low, and place a tight-fitting lid on the saucepan. Steam for about 12 minutes, or until the sweet potato cubes are tender when pierced with a fork and the chicken is cooked through (there should be no pink remaining in the center when you cut into a

piece, or use a meat thermometer to make sure the internal temperature of the chicken has reached 165°F).

Carefully remove the chicken and sweet potato, draining any excess cooking liquid. Allow the chicken and sweet potato to cool for a few minutes. Transfer it to a serving bowl, pour barbecue sauce on, stirring everything together if desired, and serve to your little one.

STORAGE INFORMATION
3 days refrigerator
2 months freezer

NOTE: These meatballs freeze well. I make 4 batches, one after the other, which uses a total of 1 pound ground turkey. To freeze the meatballs, allow them to cool completely after steaming, then place them either in a single layer or separate layers with wax paper in an airtight container or resealable freezer bag and freeze for up to 2 months. These meatballs make a delicious adult meal, too, in which case I suggest adding a pinch of kosher salt and freshly ground black pepper before serving.

baby meatballs with carrots and herbs

makes 12 small meatballs

¼ pound ground turkey

¼ large carrot, peeled and grated (1 to 2 tablespoons)

1 teaspoon grated onion

1½ teaspoons reduced-sodium soy sauce

2 teaspoons plain full-fat Greek yogurt

½ teaspoon dried parsley

These little meatballs are so good that it's mind-blowing they can be made in a baby food maker! Whenever I make these baby meatballs, my son picks them up with his little hands and gobbles them right up.

In a small bowl, combine all the ingredients and mix well. Form small meatballs using about 1 teaspoon of the mixture per meatball.

Cook the meatballs according to your preferred method below.

water level
COOKING TIME: 25 minutes

Pour water into the tank to the highest level (mine is level 3, which equals about 1 cup water).

Place the meatballs in the steamer basket or cooking compartment, gently stacking them as necessary.

Start the cooking process. When the cooking process is done, remove the steamer basket and allow the meatballs to cool for a few minutes before serving.

fillable tank
COOKING TIME: 20 minutes

Fill the water tank with water.

Place the meatballs in the blending bowl, gently stacking them as necessary.

Set the steam timer for 20 minutes. When the timer goes off, carefully remove the meatballs with tongs or a fork and allow the meatballs to cool for a few minutes before serving.

stovetop
COOKING TIME: 12 minutes

In a 2-quart saucepan set over high heat, bring 1 cup water to a boil, about 2 minutes. Add the meatballs in a single layer, reduce the heat to medium-low, and place a tight-fitting lid on the saucepan. Steam for about 10 minutes, or until the meatballs are cooked through (there should be no pink remaining in the center when you cut into one, or use a meat thermometer to make sure the internal temperature has reached 145°F).

Carefully remove the meatballs with tongs or a fork. Allow the meatballs to cool for a few minutes before serving.

STORAGE INFORMATION
3 days refrigerator
2 months freezer

baby bolognese

2 medium-large tomatoes, cored and quartered (I like vine, Roma, or heirloom tomato varieties for this)

1 ounce ground beef, crumbled into chunks

1 teaspoon finely chopped onion

1 tablespoon finely chopped carrot

1 tablespoon finely chopped celery

2 baby bella (cremini) mushrooms, cleaned and chopped

1 garlic clove, chopped

1 tablespoon tomato paste

What's the difference between a Bolognese and a Tomato Sauce (page 199)? Meat and consistency! A Bolognese sauce is full of meat and veggies. With this recipe, baby gets a wonderful array of veggies plus protein.

water level
COOKING TIME: 25 minutes

Pour water into the tank to the highest level (mine is level 3, which equals about 1 cup water).

Place all the ingredients except the tomato paste in the steamer basket or cooking compartment.

Start the cooking process. When the cooking process is done, remove the steamer basket and drain and discard the cooking liquid. Pour the contents of the steamer basket into the blending bowl, add the tomato paste, and blend. If the sauce seems a little too thick, add up to a few teaspoons water until the desired consistency is reached.

NOTE: If you have a baby food maker with an open spout, you might want to hold a paper towel or kitchen cloth over the opening when blending, so the sauce doesn't spurt out.

fillable tank
COOKING TIME: 20 minutes

Fill the water tank with water.

Place all the ingredients except the tomato paste in the blending bowl.

Set the steam timer for 20 minutes. When the timer goes off, drain and discard a little (1 to 2 tablespoons) of the cooking liquid. Add the tomato paste to the blending bowl and blend. If the sauce seems a little too thick, add up to a few teaspoons water until the desired consistency is reached.

stovetop
COOKING TIME: 13 minutes

In a 2-quart saucepan set over high heat, bring 1 cup water to a boil, about 3 minutes. Add all the ingredients except the tomato paste, reduce the heat to medium-low, and place a tight-fitting lid on the saucepan. Steam for about 10 minutes, or until the tomato pieces are very tender. Drain off a little (1 to 2 tablespoons) of the cooking liquid.

Transfer contents of the saucepan to a blender (or food processor), add the tomato paste, and blend. If the sauce seems a little too thick, add up to a few teaspoons water until desired consistency is reached.

STORAGE INFORMATION
3 days refrigerator
2 months freezer

NOTE: This goes very well over grains or whole-wheat pasta. Serve this as an adult meal by adding a generous pinch of kosher salt and topping it with freshly grated Parmesan cheese.

beef and broccoli with grain

1 ounce ground beef, crumbled into a few pieces

½ cup broccoli florets

¼ cup cooked brown rice

2 teaspoons extra-virgin olive oil

1 teaspoon low-sodium soy sauce

¼ cup no-sodium beef, chicken, or vegetable broth (optional; see Notes)

Beef and broccoli are combined with a grain and drizzled with a little olive oil and soy sauce in this recipe. I recommend making it into a very chunky puree for baby, because some of the ingredients may be a little tough for new gums to chew.

water level

COOKING TIME: 25 minutes

Pour water into the tank to the highest level (mine is level 3, which equals about 1 cup water).

Put the beef and broccoli in the steamer basket or cooking compartment.

Start the cooking process. When the cooking process is done, pour the contents of the steamer basket into the blending bowl and add the brown rice, olive oil, and soy sauce. Blend. Alternatively, drain the cooking liquid before pouring the beef and broccoli into the blending bowl. Add the broth along with the brown rice, olive oil, and soy sauce before blending until the desired consistency is reached.

fillable tank

COOKING TIME: 20 minutes

Fill the water tank with water.

Place the beef and broccoli in the blending bowl.

Set the steam timer for 20 minutes. When the timer goes off, add the brown rice, olive oil, and soy sauce to the blending bowl and blend. Alternatively, drain and discard the cooking liquid, then add the broth along with the brown rice, olive oil, and soy sauce. Blend until the desired consistency is reached.

stovetop

COOKING TIME: 13 minutes

In a 2-quart saucepan set over high heat, bring 1 cup water to a boil, about 3 minutes. Add the beef and broccoli, reduce the heat to medium-low, and place a tight-fitting lid on the saucepan. Steam for about 10 minutes, or until the beef is cooked through and the broccoli florets are easily pierced with a fork.

Transfer the beef and broccoli to a blender (or food processor) with the cooking liquid. Add the brown rice, olive oil, and soy sauce and blend. Alternatively, drain and discard the cooking liquid before transferring the beef and broccoli to the blender. Add the broth along with the brown rice, olive oil, and soy sauce and blend until the desired consistency is reached.

NOTES: Draining the cooking liquid and using broth instead offers a milder flavor and cleaner blend.

You can also make this chunkier by breaking up and mashing the drained ingredients with a fork (as pictured).

STORAGE INFORMATION
3 days refrigerator
2 months freezer

broccoli "rice" and cheddar

2 cups broccoli florets

¼ cup shredded Cheddar cheese

¼ cup no-sodium chicken or vegetable broth (optional; see Notes)

My son goes crazy over anything with broccoli in it, so I created this dish for him. The "rice" is blended broccoli and cheese, and I'm going to keep calling it "rice" as long as I can!

water level
COOKING TIME: 17 minutes

Pour water into the tank to the middle level (mine is level 2, which equals about ⅔ cup water).

Put the broccoli in the steamer basket or cooking compartment.

Start the cooking process. When the cooking process is done, pour the broccoli into the blending bowl, add the cheese, and blend. Alternatively, drain the cooking liquid before pouring the broccoli into the blending bowl. Add the cheese and broth and blend until the desired consistency is reached.

fillable tank
COOKING TIME: 15 minutes

Fill the water tank with water.

Place the broccoli in the blending bowl.

Set the steam timer for 15 minutes. When the timer goes off, add the cheese and blend. Alternatively, drain and discard the cooking liquid, add the broth along with the cheese to the blending bowl, and blend until the desired consistency is reached.

stovetop
COOKING TIME: 8 minutes

In a 2-quart saucepan set over high heat, bring ½ cup water to a boil, about 2 minutes. Add the broccoli, reduce the heat to medium-low, and place a tight-fitting lid on the saucepan. Steam for about 6 minutes, or until the broccoli florets are easily pierced with a fork.

Transfer the broccoli to a blender (or food processor) with the cooking liquid, add the cheese, and blend. Alternatively, drain and discard the cooking liquid before transferring the broccoli to the blender. Add the cheese and broth and blend until the desired consistency is reached.

NOTES: Draining the cooking liquid and using broth instead offers a milder flavor and cleaner blend.

I prefer draining the cooking liquid and blending or pulsing the broccoli with the cheese so that it is very thick and chunky. You can also drain and discard the cooking liquid, add the cheese, and mash the mixture with a fork to the desired consistency.

STORAGE INFORMATION
3 days refrigerator
2 months freezer

chicken, broccoli, and cheese

1 ounce skinless, boneless chicken breast, cut into ½- to 1-inch cubes

1 cup broccoli florets

¼ cup cooked brown rice

1 tablespoon shredded Cheddar cheese

¼ cup no-sodium chicken or vegetable broth (optional; see Notes)

There's something so comforting about the combination of chicken, broccoli, and cheese, isn't there? It reminds me of a hearty fall casserole. In this version, baby gets to enjoy this meal as a chunkier puree all blended together, or simply as small pieces of food, steamed together in this classic flavor combination!

water level
COOKING TIME: 25 minutes

Pour water into the tank to the highest level (mine is level 3, which equals about 1 cup water).

Put the chicken and broccoli in the steamer basket or cooking compartment.

Start the cooking process. When the cooking process is done, pour the contents of the steamer basket into the blending bowl, add the brown rice and cheese, and blend. Alternatively, drain and discard the cooking liquid before pouring the chicken and broccoli into the blending bowl. Add the broth along with the brown rice and cheese and blend until desired consistency is reached.

fillable tank
COOKING TIME: 20 minutes

Fill the water tank with water.

Place the chicken and broccoli in the blending bowl.

Set the steam timer for 20 minutes. When the timer goes off, add the brown rice and cheese to the blending bowl and blend. Alternatively, drain and discard the cooking liquid before adding the broth, brown rice, and cheese. Blend until the desired consistency is reached.

stovetop
COOKING TIME: 13 minutes

In a 2-quart saucepan set over high heat, bring 1 cup water to a boil about 3 minutes. Add the chicken and broccoli, reduce the heat to medium-low, and place a tight-fitting lid on the saucepan. Steam for about 10 minutes, or until the chicken cubes are cooked through (there should be no pink remaining in the center when you cut into a piece, or use a meat thermometer to make sure the internal temperature of the chicken has reached 165°F) and the broccoli florets are tender when pierced with a fork.

Transfer the chicken and broccoli to a blender (or food processor) with the cooking liquid, add the brown rice and cheese, and blend. Alternatively, drain and discard the cooking liquid before transferring the chicken and broccoli to the blender. Add the broth along with the brown rice and cheese and blend until the desired consistency is reached.

NOTES: Draining the cooking liquid and using broth instead offers a milder flavor and cleaner blend.

You can also make this chunkier by breaking up and mashing the drained ingredients with a fork.

STORAGE INFORMATION
3 days refrigerator
2 months freezer

tofu, cauliflower, and cheese

2 ounces firm tofu, cut into ½- to ¾-inch cubes and drained (about 1 cup)

1½ cups cauliflower florets

¼ cup shredded Cheddar cheese

1 teaspoon extra-virgin olive oil

¼ cup no-sodium chicken or vegetable broth (optional; see Notes)

Cheesy recipes are the best, aren't they? In this recipe, tofu and cauliflower are sprinkled with Cheddar (or made into a puree), which makes for a cheesy dish for baby that you'll want to sneak bites of as well.

water level
COOKING TIME: 25 minutes

Pour water into the tank to the highest level (mine is level 3, which equals about 1 cup water).

Put the tofu and cauliflower in the steamer basket or cooking compartment.

Start the cooking process. When the cooking process is done, pour the tofu and cauliflower into the blending bowl and add the cheese and olive oil. Blend. Alternatively, drain and discard the cooking liquid before pouring the tofu and cauliflower into the blending bowl. Add the broth along with the cheese and olive oil and blend until the desired consistency is reached.

fillable tank
COOKING TIME: 20 minutes

Fill the water tank with water.

Place the tofu and cauliflower in the blending bowl.

Set the steam timer for 20 minutes. When the timer goes off, add the cheese and olive oil to the blending bowl and blend. Alternatively, drain and discard the cooking liquid before adding the broth, cheese, and olive oil. Blend until the desired consistency is reached.

stovetop
COOKING TIME: 13 minutes

In a 2-quart saucepan set over high heat, bring 1 cup water to a boil, about 3 minutes. Add the tofu and cauliflower, reduce the heat to medium-low, and place a tight-fitting lid on the saucepan. Steam for about 10 minutes, or until the cauliflower florets are easily pierced with a fork.

Transfer the tofu and cauliflower to a blender (or food processor) with the cooking liquid, add the cheese and olive oil, and blend. Alternatively, drain and discard the cooking liquid before transferring the tofu and cauliflower to the blender. Add the broth along with the cheese and olive oil and blend until the desired consistency is reached.

NOTES: Draining the cooking liquid and using broth instead offers a milder flavor and cleaner blend.

You can also make this chunkier by breaking up and mashing the drained ingredients with a fork.

STORAGE INFORMATION
3 days refrigerator
2 months freezer

chicken, sweet potatoes, and cumin

1 ounce skinless, boneless chicken breast, cut into ½- to ¾-inch cubes

1 cup peeled and cubed sweet potato

¼ teaspoon ground cumin

If there's one seasoning my husband loves, it is cumin, so it was imperative that I start incorporating the warm and fragrant spice into our son's food as early as possible. Cumin is used frequently in Hispanic and Indian cuisines and goes perfectly in this chunkier puree. If your baby is eating solids, simply cook the chicken and sweet potatoes and sprinkle some ground cumin on top!

water level
COOKING TIME: 25 minutes

Pour water into the tank to the highest level (mine is level 3, which equals about 1 cup water).

Put the chicken and sweet potato in the steamer basket or cooking compartment.

Start the cooking process. When the cooking process is done, drain and discard a little of the cooking liquid (or all of it for a thicker puree). Pour the chicken and sweet potato into the blending bowl with the remaining cooking liquid. Add the cumin and blend until the desired consistency is reached.

fillable tank
COOKING TIME: 20 minutes

Fill the water tank with water.

Place the chicken and sweet potato in the blending bowl.

Set the steam timer for 20 minutes. When the timer goes off, drain and discard a little of the cooking liquid (or all of it for a thicker puree). Add the cumin to the blending bowl and blend until the desired consistency is reached.

stovetop
COOKING TIME: 13 minutes

In a 2-quart saucepan set over high heat, bring 1 cup water to a boil, about 3 minutes. Add the chicken and sweet potato, reduce the heat to medium-low, and place a tight-fitting lid on the saucepan. Steam for about 10 minutes, or until the chicken is cooked through (there should be no pink remaining in the center when you cut into a piece, or use a meat thermometer to make sure the internal temperature of the chicken has reached 165°F) and the sweet potato cubes are easily pierced with a fork. Drain and discard a little of the cooking liquid (or all of it for a thicker puree).

Transfer the chicken and sweet potato to a blender (or food processor) with the remaining cooking liquid, add the cumin, and blend until the desired consistency is reached.

STORAGE INFORMATION
3 days refrigerator
2 months freezer

white fish chowder

1 ounce deboned white fish, skin removed, cut into a few pieces

2 small potatoes, peeled and chopped (about ½ cup)

2 tablespoons finely chopped white or yellow onion

1 teaspoon unsalted butter

¼ cup whole milk

¼ cup no-sodium chicken broth

¼ teaspoon Old Bay seasoning or sweet paprika

Pinch of dried thyme, or ½ teaspoon chopped fresh

Pinch of dried parsley, or ½ teaspoon chopped fresh

This white fish chowder is a thick and creamy stew, a great way to introduce baby to the classic dish. I like to use halibut, cod, or snapper in this recipe, and when baby starts to eat more solids, serve it with a crumbled cracker on top!

water level
COOKING TIME: 25 minutes

Pour water into the tank to the highest level (mine is level 3, which equals about 1 cup water).

Place the fish, potato, and onion in the steamer basket or cooking compartment.

Start the cooking process. When the cooking process is done, drain and discard the cooking liquid. Pour the contents from the steamer basket into the blending bowl. Add the milk, butter, broth, and seasonings. If you want a more blended, thicker consistency, pulse for a few seconds. Allow to cool for a few minutes before serving.

NOTE: If you have a baby food maker with an open spout, you might want to hold a paper towel or kitchen cloth over the opening when blending so the liquid doesn't spurt out.

fillable tank
COOKING TIME: 25 minutes

Fill the water tank with water.

Place the fish, potato, and onion in the blending bowl.

Set the steam timer for 25 minutes. When the timer goes off, drain and discard the cooking liquid. Add the milk, butter, broth, and seasonings to the blending bowl. If you want a more blended, thicker consistency, pulse for a few seconds. Allow it to cool for a few minutes before serving.

stovetop
COOKING TIME: 13 minutes

In a 2-quart saucepan set over high heat, bring 1 cup water to a boil, about 3 minutes. Add the fish, potato, and onion; reduce the heat to medium-low; and place a tight-fitting lid on the saucepan. Steam for about

10 minutes, or until the potato cubes are easily pierced with a fork.

Drain and discard the cooking liquid.

Stir in the milk, butter, broth, and seasonings. If you want a more blended, thicker consistency, transfer the contents of the saucepan to a blender (or food processer) and pulse for a few seconds. Allow it to cool for a few minutes before serving.

NOTE: To turn this into an adult recipe, add ¼ teaspoon kosher salt and serve with oyster or saltine crackers.

STORAGE INFORMATION
3 days refrigerator
2 months freezer

ginger-tomato chicken and sweet potatoes

2 ounces chicken breast, cut into ½- to ¾-inch cubes

1 medium sweet potato, peeled and cut into ½- to ¾-inch cubes (about 1 cup)

1 small vine or Roma tomato, finely chopped

¼ teaspoon grated fresh ginger

1 teaspoon extra-virgin olive oil

For this recipe, tomato and ginger are cooked with chicken and sweet potato, making a fragrant and flavorful dish. I like to add spices such as curry, cumin, or turmeric to this dish and give it an Indian flavor profile.

water level
COOKING TIME: 25 minutes

Pour water into the tank to the highest level (mine is level 3, which equals about 1 cup water).

Place the chicken and sweet potato in the steamer basket or cooking compartment, and top with the tomato and ginger.

Start the cooking process. When the cooking process is done, transfer the chicken and sweet potato mixture to a bowl and allow it to cool a few minutes. Drizzle the olive oil on top and feed it to your little one.

fillable tank
COOKING TIME: 20 minutes

Fill the water tank with water.

Place the chicken and sweet potato in the blending bowl and top with the tomato and ginger.

Set the steam timer for 20 minutes. When the timer goes off, drain the cooking liquid, transfer the chicken and sweet potato mixture to a bowl, and allow it to cool a few minutes. Drizzle the olive oil on top and feed it to your little one.

stovetop
COOKING TIME: 14 minutes

In a 2-quart saucepan set over high heat, bring ½ cup water to a boil, about 2 minutes. Add the chicken and sweet potato, top with the tomato and ginger, reduce the heat to medium-low, and place a tight-fitting lid on the saucepan. Steam for about 12 minutes, or until the sweet potato cubes are easily pierced with a fork and the chicken is cooked through (there should be no pink remaining in the center when you cut into a piece, or use a meat thermometer to make sure the internal temperature of the chicken has reached 165°F).

Drain and discard the cooking liquid. Transfer the chicken and sweet potato mixture to a bowl and allow it to cool a few minutes. Drizzle the olive oil on top and feed it to your little one.

STORAGE INFORMATION
3 days refrigerator
2 months freezer

NOTE: This can also be made into a chunky puree by blending the ingredients with a little bit of the cooking liquid.

secretly carrot cheddar cheese sauce

1 large carrot, peeled and cut into small pieces (about ½ cup)

½ cup shredded Cheddar cheese

1 tablespoon whole-milk yogurt

A cheesy sauce that's healthy? Sign me up—and my baby! This sauce uses carrots as the base and then combines them with Cheddar cheese and yogurt in the perfect sauce for whole-wheat pasta or veggies. One of my favorite things is to make mac 'n' cheese with this sauce! My son always chooses this over the standard boxed product!

water level

COOKING TIME: 25 minutes

Pour water into the tank to the highest level (mine is level 3, which equals about 1 cup water).

Put the carrot in the steamer basket or cooking compartment.

Start the cooking process. When the cooking process is done, drain and discard the cooking liquid. Pour the carrots in the blending bowl and add the cheese, yogurt, and ¼ cup water. Blend until smooth.

fillable tank

COOKING TIME: 20 minutes

Fill the water tank with water.

Place the carrot in the blending bowl.

Set the steam timer for 20 minutes.

When the timer goes off, drain and discard the cooking liquid. Add the cheese, yogurt, and ¼ cup water to the blending bowl. Blend until smooth.

stovetop

COOKING TIME: 13 minutes

In a 2-quart saucepan set over high heat, bring the carrot and 1 cup water (or enough water to almost cover the carrots) to a boil, about 3 minutes. Reduce the heat to medium-low and place a tight-fitting lid on the saucepan. Steam for 10 minutes, or until the carrot pieces are easily pierced with a fork.

Drain and discard the cooking liquid. Transfer the carrots to a blender (or food processor), add the cheese, yogurt, and ¼ cup water, and blend until smooth.

STORAGE INFORMATION
3 days refrigerator
2 months freezer

NOTE: Turn this into an adult Cheddar cheese sauce by adding a pinch of garlic salt before blending.

cilantro lime cauliflower "rice"

1½ to 2 cups cauliflower florets

1 tablespoon finely chopped onion

1 teaspoon extra-virgin olive oil

1 teaspoon fresh lime juice

1 tablespoon finely chopped fresh cilantro

¼ teaspoon ground cumin

¼ cup no-sodium chicken or vegetable broth (optional; see Notes)

Cauliflower "rice" is finely chopped cauliflower that is used in place of actual rice. I love the cilantro rice they serve at fast-casual Mexican restaurants, and I wanted to make a fun version for babies. This goes great with a protein such as chicken, fish, or tofu.

water level
COOKING TIME: 17 minutes

Pour water into the tank to the middle level (mine is level 2, which equals about ⅔ cup water).

Put the cauliflower and onion in the steamer basket or cooking compartment.

Start the cooking process. When the cooking process is done, pour the contents of the steamer basket into the blending bowl, add the olive oil, lime juice, cilantro, and cumin, and blend. Alternatively, drain and discard the cooking liquid before pouring the cauliflower and onion in the blending bowl. Add the broth along with the remaining ingredients. Blend until the desired consistency is reached.

fillable tank
COOKING TIME: 15 minutes

Fill the water tank with water.

Place the cauliflower and onion in the blending bowl.

Set the steam timer for 15 minutes. When the timer goes off, add the olive oil, lime juice, cilantro, and cumin to the blending bowl and blend. Alternatively, drain and discard the cooking liquid and add the broth along with the remaining ingredients. Blend until the desired consistency is reached.

stovetop
COOKING TIME: 7 minutes

In a 2-quart saucepan set over high heat, bring ½ cup water to a boil, about 2 minutes. Add the cauliflower and onion, reduce the heat to medium-low, and place a tight-fitting lid on the saucepan. Steam for 5 minutes.

Transfer the cauliflower and onion to a blender (or food processor) with the cooking liquid. Add the olive oil, lime juice, cilantro, and cumin and blend. Alternatively, drain and discard the cooking liquid before transferring the cauliflower and onion to the blender. Add the broth along with the remaining ingredients and blend until the desired consistency is reached.

NOTES: Draining the cooking liquid and using broth instead offers a milder flavor and cleaner blend; you can also drain the cooking liquid and forgo the broth for a thick and chunky variation. Just two or three pulses of the drained mixture will give you a nice texture.

You can also make this chunkier by breaking up and mashing the drained ingredients with a fork (as pictured).

Turn this into an adult dish by adding ¼ teaspoon garlic salt along with the olive oil, lime juice, cilantro, and cumin before blending.

STORAGE INFORMATION
3 days refrigerator
2 months freezer

teriyaki salmon, broccoli, and brown rice

TERIYAKI SAUCE

2 tablespoons low-sodium soy sauce

1 tablespoon brown sugar

1 teaspoon pure maple syrup

¼ teaspoon grated fresh ginger

Pinch of garlic powder

SALMON, BROCCOLI, AND BROWN RICE

2 ounces deboned salmon, skin removed, cut into a few pieces

½ cup broccoli florets

¼ cup cooked brown rice

Who doesn't love a good teriyaki sauce? The rich, sweet brown sauce is a great introduction to Asian flavors. This homemade version contains less sugar and thickeners than a store-bought one, but it has a great flavor that goes with salmon, chicken, beef, or tofu, so feel free to swap out the protein in this recipe.

Make the teriyaki sauce: In a small bowl, whisk together all the sauce ingredients and set aside. The sauce can be stored in the refrigerator for up to 1 week before using in this recipe.

Cook the salmon and broccoli according to your preferred method below. Serve this as a chunky puree with all ingredients blended or as solids by breaking the foods into pieces and feeding them to baby.

water level
COOKING TIME: 25 minutes

Pour water into the tank to the highest level (mine is level 3, which equals about 1 cup water).

Place the salmon and broccoli in the steamer basket or cooking compartment.

Start the cooking process. When the cooking process is done,

remove the steamer basket and allow the salmon and broccoli to cool for a few minutes, then transfer them to a bowl with the cooked brown rice, pour on the teriyaki sauce, and feed it to your little one.

fillable tank
COOKING TIME: 25 minutes

Fill the water tank with water.

Place the salmon and broccoli in the blending bowl.

Set the steam timer for 25 minutes. When the timer goes off, carefully remove the salmon and broccoli with tongs or a fork, making sure to drain any excess cooking liquid, and transfer them to a bowl. Add the cooked brown rice and allow the salmon and broccoli to cool for a few minutes. Pour on the teriyaki sauce and feed it to your little one.

stovetop
COOKING TIME: 13 minutes

In a 2-quart saucepan set over high heat, bring 1 cup water to a boil, about 3 minutes. Add the salmon and broccoli, reduce the heat to medium-low, and place a tight-fitting lid on the saucepan. Steam for about 10 minutes, or until the broccoli florets are easily pierced with a fork and the salmon is cooked through (it shouldn't appear translucent when you break into a piece).

Remove from heat. Drain and discard any excess cooking liquid, transfer the salmon and broccoli to a bowl, and add the brown rice. Allow them to cool for a few minutes, then pour on the teriyaki sauce and serve it to your little one.

STORAGE INFORMATION
3 days refrigerator
2 months freezer

gentle baby chili

¼ pound ground beef, crumbled into pieces

½ cup cooked black beans, drained and rinsed

½ cup cooked pinto beans, drained and rinsed

½ cup cooked kidney beans, drained and rinsed

¼ small carrot, peeled and cut into pieces (about ¼ cup)

1 tablespoon finely chopped onion

¼ teaspoon chili powder

¼ teaspoon sweet paprika

¼ teaspoon garlic powder, or 1 garlic clove, pressed

¼ cup low-sodium beef broth, plus more as needed

Everyone loves a good chili, right? Well, you can make a great one for your baby too! For baby, the flavors are a little milder, and there is no salt. If you want to prepare this chili for adults, simply use a heavier hand when adding seasonings, and include salt.

water level
COOKING TIME: 25 minutes

Pour water into the tank to the highest level (mine is level 3, which equals about 1 cup water).

Place all the ingredients in the steamer basket or cooking compartment. Start the cooking process. When the cooking process is done, pour the contents of the steamer basket into the blending bowl and pulse a few times to bring the chili together. If the chili is too thick, add more broth until the desired consistency is reached.

fillable tank
COOKING TIME: 25 minutes

Fill the water tank with water.

Place all the ingredients in the blending bowl.

Set the steam timer for 25 minutes. When the timer goes off, pulse the mixture for a few seconds until the chili comes together. If the chili is too thick, add more broth until the desired consistency is reached.

stovetop
COOKING TIME: 15 minutes

In a 2-quart saucepan set over high heat, bring 1 cup water to a boil, about 3 minutes. Add all the ingredients, reduce the heat to medium-low, and place a tight-fitting lid on the saucepan. Steam for about 12 minutes, or until the ground beef is cooked through and no pink remains in the center.

Transfer the ingredients to a blender (or food processor) with the cooking liquid and blend for a few seconds until the chili comes together. If the chili is too thick, add more broth until the desired consistency is reached.

NOTE: Chili goes really well with cornbread muffins. If you're looking for a sweet-potato cornbread muffin baby and adults will love, head to sweetphi.com/extras for the recipe.

STORAGE INFORMATION
3 days refrigerator
2 months freezer

herby salmon and potatoes

1½ ounces deboned salmon, cut into a few 1-inch pieces

3 baby potatoes, peeled or unpeeled, cut into ½- to ¾-inch cubes

¼ teaspoon finely chopped fresh parsley

¼ teaspoon finely chopped fresh basil

1 teaspoon extra-virgin olive oil

⅓ cup no-sodium chicken or vegetable broth (optional; see page 156)

Salmon and potatoes is such a nutritious meal for baby, with omega-3 fatty acids that help brain and nervous system development. This is a great recipe either to puree (which is a pretty pinkish color) and feed to baby or to mash up with a fork and let your little one pick up when they're eating more solids. You can cook the salmon with or without skin, removing it, if necessary, after the fish is steamed.

water level
COOKING TIME: 25 minutes

Pour water into the tank to the highest level (mine is level 3, which equals about 1 cup water).

Place the salmon and potato in the steamer basket or cooking compartment. Sprinkle the parsley and basil over the salmon.

Start the cooking process. When the cooking process is done, remove the salmon from the steamer basket and, if necessary, take off and discard the skin. Drizzle the olive oil over the salmon. Put the salmon and the remaining contents of the steamer basket in the blending bowl and blend. Alternatively, drain and discard the cooking liquid after removing the salmon. Place the skinless salmon in the blending bowl, add the remaining contents of the steamer basket along with the broth, and blend until the desired consistency is reached.

fillable tank
COOKING TIME: 20 minutes

Fill the water tank with water.

Place the salmon and potato in the blending bowl and sprinkle the parsley and basil on top.

Set the steam timer for 20 minutes. When the timer goes off, remove the skin from the salmon (if necessary). Return the salmon to the blending bowl, drizzle with the olive oil, and blend. Alternatively, drain and discard the cooking liquid and return the skinless salmon to the blending bowl. Drizzle the olive oil on top, add the broth, and blend until the desired consistency is reached.

stovetop
COOKING TIME: 15 minutes

In a 2-quart saucepan set over high heat, bring 1 cup water to a boil, about 3 minutes. Add the salmon and potato, sprinkle the parsley and basil on top, reduce the heat to medium-low, and place a tight-fitting lid on the saucepan. Steam for about 12 minutes, or until the salmon is cooked through (it shouldn't appear translucent when you break into a piece) and the potato cubes are easily pierced with a fork.

When the ingredients are done cooking, remove the salmon from the saucepan and, if necessary, take off and discard the skin. Transfer the salmon to a blender (or food processor) with the contents of the saucepan, drizzle with the olive oil, and blend. Alternatively, drain and discard the cooking liquid before transferring the skinless salmon to the blender. Drizzle it with the olive oil and add the remaining contents of the saucepan along with the broth. Blend until the desired consistency is reached.

STORAGE INFORMATION
3 days refrigerator
2 months freezer

ground beef, peas, and potatoes

2 small yellow potatoes, peeled and cut into ½- to ¾-inch cubes (about 1 cup)

1 small carrot, cut into pieces (about ½ cup)

¼ cup frozen peas

¼ pound ground beef, crumbled

¼ teaspoon dried parsley

¼ teaspoon garlic powder, or 1 garlic clove, pressed

⅓ cup no-sodium beef, chicken, or vegetable broth (optional; see Notes)

My husband calls this "baby stew" because it does in fact look and smell like a wonderful Irish stew! This can be made into a puree by blending it longer, or serve it as an almost puree-soft food by blending it just a little and leaving a few tender, larger pieces. I like adding a few herbs and spices, like parsley and garlic powder, to really amp up the flavor.

water level
COOKING TIME: 25 minutes

Pour water into the tank to the highest level (mine is level 3, which equals about 1 cup water).

Place the potato, carrot, and peas in the steamer basket or cooking compartment and crumble the ground beef on top. Sprinkle the parsley and garlic powder over the ground beef.

Start the cooking process. When the cooking process is done, pour the contents of the steamer basket with the cooking liquid into the blending bowl and blend. Alternatively, drain and discard the cooking liquid before pouring the contents into the blending bowl, then add the broth and blend until the desired consistency is reached.

fillable tank
COOKING TIME: 25 minutes

Fill the water tank with water.

Place the potato, carrot, and peas in the blending bowl, and crumble the ground beef on top. Sprinkle the parsley and garlic powder over the ground beef.

Set the steam timer for 25 minutes. When the timer goes off, blend the contents with the cooking liquid. Alternatively, drain and discard the cooking liquid, add the broth, and blend until the desired consistency is reached.

stovetop
COOKING TIME: 15 minutes

In a 2-quart saucepan set over high heat, bring 1 cup water to a boil, about 3 minutes. Add the potato, carrot, and peas and crumble the ground beef on top. Reduce the heat to medium-low and place a tight-fitting lid on the saucepan. Steam for about 12 minutes, or until the potato cubes are easily pierced with a fork and the ground beef is cooked through and no pink remains in the center.

Sprinkle the dried parsley and garlic powder over the contents in the saucepan.

Transfer the ingredients to a blender (or food processor) with the cooking liquid and process. Alternatively, drain and discard the cooking liquid before transferring the ingredients to a blender, add the broth, and blend until the desired consistency is reached.

NOTES: You could also use a pinch of dried or chopped fresh rosemary, thyme, or oregano before blending.

Draining the cooking liquid and using broth instead offers a milder flavor and cleaner blend.

STORAGE INFORMATION
3 days refrigerator
2 months freezer

indian-spiced sweet potatoes and carrots

1 cup peeled and cubed sweet potato

1 large carrot, peeled and cut into ½- to ¾-inch slices (about ½ cup)

¼ teaspoon ground cardamom

¼ teaspoon curry powder

I love knowing that I'm doing the right things to raise an adventurous eater. I introduce new spices to my son by pairing them with foods he already loves, like sweet potatoes and carrots. In this Indian-spiced dish, dashes of warming cardamom and curry are used.

water level
COOKING TIME: 25 minutes

Pour water into the tank to the highest level (mine is level 3, which equals about 1 cup water).

Put the sweet potato and carrot in the steamer basket or cooking compartment.

Start the cooking process. When the cooking process is done, pour the sweet potato and carrot into the blending bowl with the cooking liquid, add the cardamom and curry powder, and blend.

fillable tank
COOKING TIME: 25 minutes

Fill the water tank with water.

Place the sweet potato and carrot in the blending bowl.

Set the steam timer for 25 minutes. When the timer goes off, add the cardamom and curry powder and blend.

stovetop
COOKING TIME: 13 minutes

In a 2-quart saucepan set over high heat, bring 1 cup water to a boil, about 3 minutes. Add the sweet potato and carrot, reduce the heat to medium-low, and place a tight-fitting lid on the saucepan. Steam for about 10 minutes, or until the sweet potato cubes are easily pierced with a fork.

Transfer the sweet potato and carrot to a blender (or food processor) with the cooking liquid, add the cardamom and curry powder, and blend.

NOTE: **This dish would be great with a protein or over grains. Add 1 ounce cooked chicken, fish, or beef either before or after steaming. This can also be made into a chunkier puree by draining and discarding the cooking liquid. Or give baby the spiced cubes of sweet potato and carrot to pick up and enjoy on their own.**

STORAGE INFORMATION
3 days refrigerator
2 months freezer

lemony quinoa chicken

1 ounce skinless, boneless chicken, cut into ½- to ¾-inch cubes

¼ cup chopped carrots

¼ cup chopped celery

¼ cup cooked quinoa

1 teaspoon lemon juice

2 teaspoons extra-virgin olive oil

¼ teaspoon dried dill

¼ teaspoon dried thyme or parsley

¼ cup no-sodium chicken or vegetable broth (optional; see Notes)

Lemony quinoa chicken can be served as a wonderful thick puree or even as a stew. It is super comforting, reminiscent of chicken soup.

water level
COOKING TIME: 25 minutes

Pour water into the tank to the highest level (mine is level 3, which equals about 1 cup water).

Put the chicken, carrot, and celery in the steamer basket or cooking compartment.

Start the cooking process. When the cooking process is done, pour the contents of the steamer basket into the blending bowl; add the quinoa, lemon juice, olive oil, and herbs; and blend. Alternatively, drain and discard the cooking liquid, then pour the remaining contents of the steamer basket into the blending bowl; add the quinoa, olive oil, herbs, and broth; and blend until the desired consistency is reached.

fillable tank
COOKING TIME: 20 minutes

Fill the water tank with water.

Place the chicken, carrot, and celery in the blending bowl.

Set the steam timer for 20 minutes. When the timer goes off, add the quinoa, olive oil, and herbs to the blending bowl and blend. Alternatively, drain and discard the cooking liquid. Add the broth along with the quinoa, lemon juice, olive oil, and herbs and blend until the desired consistency is reached.

stovetop
COOKING TIME: 13 minutes

In a 2-quart saucepan set over high heat, bring 1 cup water to a boil, about 3 minutes. Add the chicken, carrot, and celery; reduce the heat to medium-low; and place a tight-fitting lid on the saucepan. Steam for about 10 minutes, or until the chicken is cooked through (there should be no pink remaining in the center when you cut into a piece, or use a meat thermometer to make sure the internal temperature of the chicken has reached 165°F) and the carrot and celery pieces are easily pierced with a fork.

Transfer the contents of the saucepan to a blender (or food processor) with the cooking liquid; add the quinoa, lemon juice, olive oil, and herbs; and blend. Alternatively, drain and discard the cooking liquid before transferring the contents to the blender. Add the broth along with the quinoa, olive, oil, and herbs and blend until the desired consistency is reached.

NOTES: Draining the cooking liquid and using broth instead offers a milder flavor and cleaner blend.

To serve this as a chunkier baby food or stew, add the quinoa, olive oil, and herbs to the steamed and drained chicken, carrot, and celery and mash the ingredients together with a fork as desired.

STORAGE INFORMATION
3 days refrigerator
2 months freezer

salmon, apricot, and sweet potatoes

1½ ounces deboned salmon, cut into a few 1-inch pieces

1 apricot, pitted and cut into a few large pieces

1 cup peeled and cubed sweet potato

1 teaspoon extra-virgin olive oil

¼ teaspoon sweet paprika

⅓ cup no-sodium chicken or vegetable broth (optional; see Note)

This recipe is a great way to serve fish to your little one. As your baby transitions to solids, you can leave this puree a little chunkier.

water level
COOKING TIME: 25 minutes

Pour water into the tank to the highest level (mine is level 3, which equals about 1 cup water).

Place the salmon, apricot, and sweet potato in the steamer basket or cooking compartment.

Start the cooking process. When the cooking process is done, remove the salmon from the steamer basket and, if necessary, take off and discard the skin. Drizzle the olive oil over the salmon and sprinkle with paprika. Put the salmon and the remaining contents of the steamer basket in the blending bowl and blend. Alternatively, drain and discard the cooking liquid after removing but before seasoning the salmon. Place the salmon and the remaining contents of the steamer basket in the blending bowl. Add the broth and blend until the desired consistency is reached.

fillable tank
COOKING TIME: 20 minutes

Fill the water tank with water.

Place the salmon, apricot, and sweet potato in the blending bowl.

Set the steam timer for 20 minutes. When the timer goes off, remove the skin from the salmon, if necessary. Return the salmon to the blending bowl, drizzle with the olive oil, sprinkle with the paprika, and blend. Alternatively, drain and discard the cooking liquid after removing and seasoning the salmon. Return the salmon to the blending bowl, drizzle with the olive oil, and sprinkle the paprika on top. Add the broth and blend until the desired consistency is reached.

stovetop
COOKING TIME: 15 minutes

In a 2-quart saucepan set over high heat, bring 1 cup water to a boil, about 3 minutes. Add the salmon, apricot, and sweet potato; reduce the heat to medium-low; and place a tight-fitting lid on the saucepan. Steam for about 12 minutes, or until the salmon is cooked through (it shouldn't appear translucent when you break into a piece) and the sweet potato cubes are easily pierced with a fork.

If necessary, remove the skin from the salmon. Transfer the contents of the saucepan and the skinless salmon to a blender (or food processor) with the cooking liquid, add the olive oil and paprika, and blend. Alternatively, drain and discard the cooking liquid before transferring the salmon, apricot, and sweet potato to the blender. Add the broth along with the olive oil and paprika and blend until the desired consistency is reached.

STORAGE INFORMATION
3 days refrigerator
2 months freezer

NOTE: Draining the cooking liquid and using broth instead offers a milder flavor and cleaner blend.

NOTES: Draining the cooking liquid and using broth instead offers a milder flavor and cleaner blend.

This also makes a great steamed-vegetable side dish for the family. Simply add a sprinkle of kosher salt and freshly ground pepper before serving.

To prepare this as finger food, drain and discard the cooking liquid, and, if necessary, cut the vegetables into smaller pieces. Stir in the lemon juice and olive oil, and serve to your little one.

lemony zucchini, asparagus, and green beans

½ cup (1-inch pieces) trimmed green beans (about 3 ounces)

¾ cup chopped zucchini, peeled or unpeeled

¾ cup trimmed and chopped asparagus

1 teaspoon fresh lemon juice

1 teaspoon extra-virgin olive oil

¼ cup no-sodium chicken or vegetable broth (optional; see Notes)

When your baby is starting solids, this steamed combination of veggies is a great transition recipe. It can be served as a puree or a chunkier puree, or as little pieces.

water level

COOKING TIME: 17 minutes

Pour water into the tank to the middle level (mine is level 2, which equals about ⅔ cup water).

Put the green beans, zucchini, and asparagus in the steamer basket or cooking compartment.

Start the cooking process. When the cooking process is done, pour the contents of the steamer basket into the blending bowl, add the lemon juice and olive oil, and blend. Alternatively, drain and discard the cooking liquid before pouring the green beans, zucchini, and asparagus into the blending bowl. Add the broth along with the lemon juice and olive oil and blend until the desired consistency is reached.

fillable tank

COOKING TIME: 15 minutes

Fill the water tank with water.

Place the green beans, zucchini, and asparagus in the blending bowl.

Set the steam timer for 15 minutes. When the timer goes off, add the lemon juice and olive oil to the blending bowl and blend. Alternatively, drain and discard the cooking liquid before adding the broth along with the lemon juice and olive oil. Blend until the desired consistency is reached.

stovetop

COOKING TIME: 8 minutes

In a 2-quart saucepan set over high heat, bring ½ cup of water to a boil, about 2 minutes. Add the green beans, zucchini, and asparagus; reduce the heat to medium-low; and place a tight-fitting lid on the saucepan. Steam for about 6 minutes.

Transfer the contents of the saucepan to a blender (or food processor) with the cooking liquid, add the lemon juice and olive oil, and blend. Alternatively, drain and discard the cooking liquid before transferring the contents to the blender. Add the broth along with the lemon juice and olive oil and blend until the desired consistency is reached.

STORAGE INFORMATION
3 days refrigerator
2 months freezer

potato leek soup

2 small yellow potatoes, peeled and cut into cubes (about 1 cup)

1 well-cleaned and chopped leek (white and light green parts only)

½ cup whole milk

1 tablespoon unsalted butter

¼ teaspoon garlic powder

Leeks and potatoes combine to make a smooth, thick, and creamy soup that reminds me of cozy weekends in the autumn and early winter. Leeks taste like a milder onion, and combined with potatoes, they have a subtle, tangy flavor. In the late fall, I love making a batch of this and taking it to work for lunch!

water level
COOKING TIME: 25 minutes

Pour water into the tank to the highest level (mine is level 3, which equals about 1 cup water).

Place the potato and leek in the steamer basket or cooking compartment.

Start the cooking process. When the cooking process is done, pour the contents from the steamer basket into the blending bowl and add the milk, butter, and garlic powder. Blend until smooth. Allow it to cool for a few minutes before serving.

NOTE: **If you have a baby food maker with an open spout, you might want to hold a paper towel or kitchen cloth over the opening when blending so the liquid doesn't spurt out.**

fillable tank
COOKING TIME: 20 minutes

Fill the water tank with water.

Place the potato and leek into the blending bowl.

Set the steam timer for 20 minutes. When the timer goes off, add the milk, butter, and garlic powder to the blending bowl and blend until smooth. Allow it to cool for a few minutes before serving.

stovetop
COOKING TIME: 13 minutes

In a 2-quart saucepan set over high heat, bring 1 cup water to a boil, about 3 minutes. Add the potato and leek, reduce the heat to medium-low, and place a tight-fitting lid on the saucepan. Steam for about 10 minutes, or until the potato cubes are easily pierced with a fork.

Transfer the potato and leek to a blender (or food processer) with the cooking liquid. Add the milk, butter, and garlic powder and blend until smooth. Allow it to cool for a few minutes before serving.

STORAGE INFORMATION
3 days refrigerator
2 months freezer

NOTE: **This soup easily becomes an adult recipe by stirring in ¼ teaspoon kosher salt before serving.**

savory apple-turkey meatballs

makes 12 small meatballs

¼ pound ground turkey

¼ medium apple, peeled and grated (you can use a cheese grater)

1 teaspoon grated onion

1 tablespoon plain whole-fat yogurt

¼ teaspoon ground allspice

1 teaspoon fresh orange juice

Anytime you combine apple and turkey, it's like welcoming fall into your house, but these apple and turkey meatballs are super delicious any season of the year. Baby will love the combination of sweet apple shreds mixed with savory turkey and a dash of allspice for seasoning.

In a small bowl, combine all the ingredients and mix well. Form small meatballs using about 1 teaspoon of the mixture. Cook the meatballs according to your preferred method below.

water level

COOKING TIME: 25 minutes

Pour water into the tank to the highest level (mine is level 3, which equals about 1 cup water).

Place the meatballs in the steamer basket or cooking compartment, gently stacking them as necessary.

Start the cooking process. When the cooking process is done, remove the steamer basket and allow the meatballs to cool for a few minutes before serving.

fillable tank

COOKING TIME: 20 minutes

Fill the water tank with water.

Place the meatballs in the blending bowl, gently stacking them as necessary.

Set the steam timer for 20 minutes. When the timer goes off, carefully remove the meatballs with tongs or a fork and allow them to cool a few minutes before serving.

stovetop

COOKING TIME: 12 minutes

In a 2-quart saucepan set over high heat, bring ½ cup water to a boil, about 2 minutes. Place the meatballs in a single layer in the saucepan, reduce the heat to medium-low, and place a tight-fitting lid on the saucepan. Steam for about 10 minutes, or until the meatballs are cooked through (there should be no pink in the center when you cut into one).

Carefully remove the meatballs with tongs or a fork. Allow them to cool for a few minutes before serving.

NOTE: These meatballs freeze well. I make 4 batches, which uses 1 pound ground turkey. To freeze the meatballs, allow them to cool, then place them either in a single layer or separate layers with wax paper in an airtight container or resealable freezer bag and freeze for up to 2 months. These meatballs make a delicious adult meal, too, in which case I would add a pinch of kosher salt and freshly ground pepper before serving.

STORAGE INFORMATION
3 days refrigerator
2 months freezer

slightly balsamic apple, chicken, and potatoes

2 ounces skinless, boneless chicken breast, cut into ½- to ¾-inch cubes

¼ medium apple, peeled, cored, and cut into ½- to ¾-inch cubes (about ¼ cup)

1 small potato, peeled and cut into ½- to ¾-inch cubes

½ teaspoon balsamic vinegar

1 teaspoon extra-virgin olive oil

I love the flavor combination of balsamic vinegar with apples, chicken, and potatoes. For this baby food, only a dash of balsamic is used, because you want baby to gradually become accustomed to its flavor. Once baby has tried this a few times, feel free to add more balsamic vinegar!

water level
COOKING TIME: 25 minutes

Pour water into the tank to the highest level (mine is level 3, which equals about 1 cup water).

Put the chicken, apple, and potato in the steamer basket or cooking compartment, and pour the balsamic vinegar over the top.

Start the cooking process. When the cooking process is done, remove the steamer basket and allow the chicken, apple, and potato to cool for a few minutes; discard the cooking liquid. Drizzle the olive oil on top and feed it to your little one.

fillable tank
COOKING TIME: 20 minutes

Fill the water tank with water.

Place the chicken, apple, and potato in the blending bowl and pour the balsamic vinegar over the top.

Set the steam timer for 20 minutes. When the timer goes off, drain and discard the cooking liquid. Allow the chicken, apple, and potato to cool for a few minutes, then drizzle the olive oil on top and feed it to your little one.

stovetop
COOKING TIME: 14 minutes

In a 2-quart saucepan set over high heat, bring ½ cup water to a boil, about 2 minutes. Add the chicken, apple, potato, and balsamic vinegar; reduce the heat to medium-low; and place a tight-fitting lid on the saucepan. Steam for about 12 minutes, or until the apple and potato cubes are easily pierced with a fork and the chicken is cooked through (there should be no pink remaining in the center when you cut into a piece, or use a meat thermometer to make sure the internal temperature of the chicken has reached 165°F).

Drain and discard the cooking liquid. Allow the chicken, apple, and potato to cool for a few minutes, then pour the olive oil on top and feed it to your little one.

STORAGE INFORMATION
3 days refrigerator
2 months freezer

NOTE: This can also be made into a chunky puree by blending the ingredients with a little bit of the cooking liquid.

basil, tomato, and winter squash soup

½ cup cubed winter squash or sweet potato

3 Roma or vine tomatoes, cored and quartered lengthwise

¼ teaspoon garlic powder

2 fresh basil leaves, chopped, or ½ teaspoon dried basil

Whenever I make my son this fresh, creamy soup, I snitch a spoonful (okay, fine, I snitch a few spoonfuls). When your baby starts solids, this is a great soup to serve with a side of soft grilled cheese. You can use sweet potato in place of squash in this recipe.

water level

COOKING TIME: 25 minutes

Pour water into the tank to the highest level (mine is level 3, which equals about 1 cup water).

Place the squash and tomato in the steamer basket or cooking compartment.

Start the cooking process. When the cooking process is done, pour the squash and tomato into the blending bowl with the cooking liquid. Add the garlic powder and basil. Blend until smooth. Allow the soup to cool for a few minutes before serving.

NOTE: If you have a baby food maker with an open spout, you might want to hold a paper towel or kitchen cloth over the opening when blending so the liquid doesn't spurt out.

fillable tank

COOKING TIME: 20 minutes

Fill the water tank with water.

Place the squash and tomato in the blending bowl.

Set the steam timer for 20 minutes. When the timer goes off, add the garlic powder and basil to the blending bowl. Blend until smooth. Allow the soup to cool for a few minutes before serving.

stovetop

COOKING TIME: 13 minutes

In a 2-quart saucepan set over high heat, bring 1 cup water to a boil, about 3 minutes. Add the squash and tomato, reduce the heat to medium-low, and place a tight-fitting lid on the saucepan. Steam for about 10 minutes, or until the squash cubes are easily pierced with a fork.

Transfer the squash and tomato to a blender (or food processer) with the cooking liquid, add the garlic powder and basil, and blend until smooth. Allow the soup to cool for a few minutes before serving.

NOTES: Add the basil at the end, because fresh basil tends to stay greener and be more flavorful when added after food has been cooked!

To turn this into an adult recipe, sprinkle a pinch or two of kosher salt on top.

STORAGE INFORMATION
3 days refrigerator
2 months freezer

turmeric potatoes and chicken

2 ounces skinless, boneless chicken breast, cut into ½- to ¾-inch cubes

2 small yellow potatoes, peeled and cut into ½- to ¾-inch cubes (¾ to 1 cup)

1 teaspoon extra-virgin olive oil

¼ teaspoon ground turmeric

⅓ cup no-sodium chicken or vegetable broth (optional; see Notes)

Turmeric is such a wonderful spice. Bright yellow in color, it's a natural mood booster, a great source of antioxidants, and an anti-inflammatory. Turmeric Potatoes and Chicken might sound a little exotic for a baby, but trust me, they love exploring new flavors. Serve with a side of Green Bean, Kale, and Pea Puree (page 80).

water level
COOKING TIME: 25 minutes

Pour water into the tank to the highest level (mine is level 3, which equals about 1 cup water).

Place the chicken and potato in the steamer basket or cooking compartment.

Start the cooking process. When the cooking process is done, pour the chicken and potato into the blending bowl with the cooking liquid. Add the olive oil and turmeric, and blend. Alternatively, drain and discard the cooking liquid before pouring the chicken and potato into the blending bowl. Add the broth along with the olive oil and turmeric and blend to the desired consistency.

fillable tank
COOKING TIME: 25 minutes

Fill the water tank with water.

Place the chicken and potato in the blending bowl.

Set the steam timer for 25 minutes. When the timer goes off, add the olive oil and turmeric to the blending bowl and blend. Alternatively, drain and discard the cooking liquid. Add the broth along with the olive oil and turmeric and blend until the desired consistency is reached.

stovetop
COOKING TIME: 15 minutes

In a 2-quart saucepan set over high heat, bring 1 cup water to a boil, about 3 minutes. Add the chicken and potato, reduce the heat to medium-low, and place a tight-fitting lid on the saucepan. Steam for about 12 minutes, or until the potato cubes are easily pierced with a fork.

When the ingredients are done cooking, transfer the contents of the saucepan to a blender (or food processor) with the cooking liquid, add the olive oil and turmeric, and blend. Alternatively, drain and discard the cooking liquid before transferring the contents of the saucepan to the blender. Add the broth along with the olive oil and turmeric and blend until the desired consistency is reached.

NOTES: Draining the cooking liquid and using broth instead offers a milder flavor and cleaner blend.
 You can also serve this as a chunkier baby food by breaking up and mashing the drained ingredients together with a fork.
 In addition to eating this with a green puree on the side, my son also likes plain yogurt with this meal.

STORAGE INFORMATION
3 days refrigerator
2 months freezer

tuscan white bean soup

1 (15-ounce) can white beans, such as cannellini, drained and rinsed

1 tablespoon chopped onion

1 carrot, cut into small pieces (about ½ cup)

1 kale leaf, stem removed, chopped into small pieces

Pinch of dried oregano

Pinch of dried parsley, or ½ teaspoon chopped fresh

⅔ cup no-sodium chicken broth

White beans are cooked to soft perfection with carrots, kale, and herbs in this Tuscan-inspired soup. I like making soups a little chunkier for baby, because we all know they are not the neatest eaters.

water level
COOKING TIME: 25 minutes

Pour water into the tank to the highest level (mine is level 3, which equals about 1 cup water).

Place the beans, onion, carrot, and kale in the steamer basket or cooking compartment.

Start the cooking process. When the cooking process is done, drain and discard the cooking liquid. Pour the remaining contents of the steamer basket into the blending bowl and add the herbs and broth. If you want a more blended, thicker, consistency, blend for a few seconds to puree some of the beans. Allow it to cool for a few minutes before serving.

NOTE: If you have a baby food maker with an open spout, you might want to hold a paper towel or kitchen cloth over the opening when blending so the liquid doesn't spurt out.

fillable tank
COOKING TIME: 20 minutes

Fill the water tank with water.

Place the beans, onion, carrot, and kale in the blending bowl.

Set the steam timer for 20 minutes. When the timer goes off, drain and discard the cooking liquid. Add the herbs and broth. If you want a more blended, thicker consistency, blend for a few seconds to puree some of the beans. Allow it to cool for a few minutes before serving.

stovetop
COOKING TIME: 15 minutes

In a 2-quart saucepan set over high heat, bring 1 cup water to a boil, about 3 minutes. Add the beans, onion, carrot, and kale; reduce the heat to medium-low; and place a tight-fitting lid on the saucepan. Steam for about 12 minutes, or until the carrot pieces are easily pierced with a fork.

Drain and discard the cooking liquid and add the herbs and broth. If you want a more blended, thicker consistency, transfer the contents of the saucepan to a blender (or food processer) and pulse for a few seconds to puree some of the beans. Allow it to cool for a few minutes before serving.

NOTE: To prepare this as an adult recipe, reserve and use ½ cup of the cooking liquid to make it more brothy, add ½ teaspoon kosher salt, and top with grated Parmesan cheese.

STORAGE INFORMATION
3 days refrigerator
2 months freezer

beyond baby

In this chapter, you'll find recipes for how adults can use the baby food maker! These recipes are also suitable bites for baby as they become better with chewing.

There are so many ways to use the baby food maker beyond purees! For example, the Yogurt Parfaits with Apple-Pear-Cinnamon Sauce (page 183) are a weekly breakfast in our house because they are so good, as are sandwiches made with Chickpea–Sweet Potato Spread (page 187). And whenever we have guests stay the night, I make a batch of Strawberry Sauce (page 190) for pancakes or ice cream! The baby food maker doesn't have to be just another kitchen appliance sitting unused on the counter after you're done making baby food; it's a wonderful appliance that I personally have used well beyond baby food, and I hope you will too.

A handful of recipes in this chapter can only be made using a baby food maker that includes a steamer basket. By that I am referring to a baby food maker with a basket into which a small ramekin can fit. At this time, I've only seen the steamer basket style in the makers that function via water levels, so if you have a fillable tank model, skip these recipes. And even if you have a water levels model, you should make sure that you have a steamer basket before planning to make these recipes. I tested these in the Béaba Babycook, but other models are coming on the market all the time, and these recipes should work in any water level device with a steamer basket.

Asparagus Pesto 181

Yogurt Parfaits with Apple-Pear-Cinnamon Sauce 183

Cheaters' Berry Crumble 184

Chickpea–Sweet Potato Spread 187

Berry Granola Parfait 188

Edamame Dip 189

Strawberry Sauce 190

Lentil Curry 193

Mango Pear Chutney 194

Mashed Garlic Herb Potatoes 196

Mashed Sweet Potatoes 197

Tomato Sauce 199

Sun-Dried Tomato Spread 200

White Bean and Garlic Dip 202

Banana-Carrot Cake (Water Level Devices with Steamer Basket Only) 203

Banana Bread (Water Level Devices with Steamer Basket Only) 205

Baby Spice Cake (Water Level Devices with Steamer Basket Only) 206

Baby Scrambled Egg Cup (Water Level Devices with Steamer Basket Only) 207

Baby Vanilla Cupcake (Water Level Devices with Steamer Basket Only) 209

Chocolate Cakelette (Water Level Devices with Steamer Basket Only) 210

asparagus pesto

makes 1 cup

1 cup (2-inch pieces) raw asparagus tips

1 teaspoon lemon zest (from 1 lemon)

Juice of ½ lemon

¼ cup Parmesan cheese

1 tablespoon chopped walnuts (optional)

2 tablespoons extra-virgin olive oil

Pinch of kosher salt

Pinch of freshly ground pepper

This pesto can be used in many ways: as a topping for your morning eggs, as a spread on your sandwich, over pasta for a quick meal, or as a pizza topping. The mild flavor of raw asparagus is amped up with lemon and olive oil. Nuts in this pesto are optional. I've made it at various times with and without nuts; both are equally tasty. This recipe is made the same way in any baby food maker, so whatever type you have, follow the first column below. But you can also make it using a blender or food processor.

baby food maker

In the blending bowl of a baby food maker, combine all the ingredients with ¼ cup water. Blend until the mixture is almost smooth but with a few small pieces remaining. Remove from the blender and enjoy!

blender or food processor

In a blender or food processor, combine all the ingredients with ¼ cup water. Blend until the mixture is almost smooth but with a few small pieces remaining. Remove from the blender and enjoy!

yogurt parfaits with apple-pear-cinnamon sauce

makes 2 parfaits

1 medium apple, peeled, cored, and cut into ½- to ¾-inch pieces (about 1 cup)

1 ripe or slightly ripe pear, peeled, cored, and cut into ½- to ¾-inch pieces (about 1 cup)

½ teaspoon ground cinnamon

1 cup plain full-fat yogurt

½ cup granola

This yogurt parfait is like eating a healthy (and still crazy delicious) version of apple crisp. I usually end up making a double batch and give the puree to my son (I omit the granola for him). This recipe also makes the best applesauce ever; it's slightly sweeter than regular applesauce because of the pear, and the cinnamon gives it a warm fall-like quality that is just sheer perfection. This is one healthy breakfast I don't mind eating repeatedly.

water level

Pour water into the tank to the highest level (mine is level 3, which equals about 1 cup water).

Put the apple and pear in the steamer basket or cooking compartment.

Start the cooking process. When the cooking process is done, drain and discard the cooking liquid. Pour the apple, pear, and cinnamon into the blending bowl. Blend for 10 seconds; it's okay if a few chunks remain. Allow it to cool before using.

To make the parfait, layer the yogurt, apple-pear sauce, and granola in a bowl and enjoy.

fillable tank

Fill the water tank with water.

Place the apple and pear in the blending bowl.

Set the steam timer for 15 minutes. When the cooking process is done, drain and discard the cooking liquid. Add the cinnamon to the blending bowl and blend for 10 seconds; it's okay if a few chunks remain. Allow it to cool before using.

To make the parfait, layer the yogurt, apple-pear sauce, and granola in a bowl and enjoy.

stovetop

In a 2-quart saucepan set over high heat, bring 1 cup water to a boil, about 3 minutes. Add the apple and pear, reduce the heat to medium-low, and place a tight-fitting lid on the saucepan. Steam for about 10 minutes, or until the apple pieces are easily pierced with a fork. Drain and discard the cooking liquid.

Transfer the apple and pear to a blender (or food processor) and add the cinnamon. Blend for 10 seconds; it's okay if a few chunks remain. Allow it to cool before using.

To make the parfait, layer the yogurt, apple-pear sauce, and granola in a bowl and enjoy.

NOTE: **You can make the apple-pear-cinnamon puree the day or night before serving so that it is cold and ready to use for the parfaits.**

cheaters'
berry
crumble

serves 2 (or 1 if you're not in the mood for sharing)

3 cups berries (I use raspberries, blueberries, and blackberries)

2 tablespoons brown sugar

½ teaspoon pure vanilla extract

1 teaspoon lemon zest

½ cup granola

Vanilla ice cream, for serving

If you're looking to impress with a super last-minute dessert that only takes a few minutes to prepare, this is the recipe you've been waiting for. This version takes only about 10 minutes to put together!

water level

Pour water into the tank to the lowest level (mine is level 1, which equals about ⅓ cup water).

Put the berries in the steamer basket or cooking compartment.

Start the cooking process. When the cooking process is done, drain and discard the cooking liquid. Pour the berries, 1 tablespoon of the brown sugar, vanilla, and lemon zest into the blending bowl. Blend very briefly, for only 2 seconds; you just want some of the berries to blend.

To make the crumbles, divide the berries between 2 bowls, top each bowl with ¼ cup granola, and evenly sprinkle the remaining 1 tablespoon brown sugar on top of the granola. Serve with vanilla ice cream and enjoy.

fillable tank

Fill the water tank with water.

Place the berries in the blending bowl.

Set the steam timer for 5 minutes. When the cooking process is done, drain and discard the cooking liquid. Pour the berries, 1 tablespoon of the brown sugar, vanilla, and lemon zest into the blending bowl. Blend very briefly, for only 2 seconds; you just want some of the berries to blend.

To make the crumbles, divide the berries between 2 bowls, top each bowl with ¼ cup granola, and evenly sprinkle the remaining 1 tablespoon brown sugar on top of the granola. Serve with vanilla ice cream and enjoy.

stovetop

In a small 2-quart saucepan set over high heat, bring ½ cup water (about ½ inch) to a boil, about 2 minutes. Add the berries, reduce the heat to medium-low, and place a tight-fitting lid on the saucepan. Steam for about 2 minutes, or until the berries are easily crushed with the back of a spoon. Drain and discard the cooking liquid.

Transfer the berries to a blender (or food processor) and add 1 tablespoon of the brown sugar, vanilla, and lemon zest. Blend very briefly, for only 2 seconds; you just want some of the berries to blend.

To make the crumbles, divide the berries between 2 bowls, top each bowl with ¼ cup granola, and evenly sprinkle the remaining 1 tablespoon brown sugar on top of the granola. Serve with vanilla ice cream and enjoy.

chickpea–sweet potato spread

makes 1½ cups

⅓ cup peeled and cubed sweet potato

1 (15-ounce) can chickpeas, drained and rinsed

1 tablespoon tahini or extra-virgin olive oil

1 garlic clove, chopped

Juice of ½ lemon (about 1 tablespoon)

¼ teaspoon kosher salt

While I don't eat an exclusively vegetarian diet, I have a lot of friends and family who do, so I'm always on the lookout for good vegetarian options. This spread is by far my favorite vegetarian sandwich spread ever. It's like a lighter, fluffier, tastier version of hummus. It is super portable and a fantastic option for picnics or an on-the-go lunch that doesn't need refrigeration. Lettuce or spinach, bell peppers, and cucumbers are my favorite sandwich or wrap fillings to use with it.

water level

Pour water into the tank to the highest level (mine is level 3, which equals about 1 cup water).

Place the sweet potato and chickpeas in the steamer basket or cooking compartment.

Start the cooking process. When the cooking process is done, pour the sweet potato and chickpeas into the blending bowl with the cooking liquid and add the remaining ingredients. Blend until thick and chunky. You may have to scrape down the sides of the bowl a few times when blending for a smoother consistency. Allow it to cool and refrigerate until ready to use as a spread or dip.

fillable tank

Fill the water tank with water.

Place the sweet potato and chickpeas in the blending bowl.

Set the steam timer for 20 minutes. When the timer goes off, add the remaining ingredients. Blend until thick and chunky. You may have to scrape down the sides of the bowl a few times when blending for a smoother consistency. Allow it to cool and refrigerate until ready to use as a spread or dip.

stovetop

In a 2 quart saucepan set over high heat, bring ½ cup water to a boil, about 2 minutes. Add the sweet potato and chickpeas, reduce the heat to medium-low, and place a tight-fitting lid on the saucepan. Steam for about 10 minutes, or until the sweet potato cubes are easily pierced with a fork.

Transfer the sweet potato and chickpeas to a blender (or food processor) with the cooking liquid. Add the remaining ingredients. Blend until thick and chunky. You may have to scrape down the sides of the blender a few times when blending for a smoother consistency. Allow it to cool and refrigerate until ready to use as a spread or dip.

NOTE: **This will keep refrigerated, covered or in an airtight container, for up to 1 week.**

berry granola parfait

serves 1

1½ cups berries (I use raspberries, blueberries, and blackberries)

1 teaspoon sugar

1 cup plain full-fat Greek yogurt

½ cup granola

Bring a little brightness to your morning yogurt and granola with this thick berry puree! I prefer this homemade version over store-bought any day. If you're looking to mix up your mornings, I'd suggest trying a ricotta breakfast bowl—just use ricotta instead of yogurt! This sauce is excellent served either hot or cold.

water level

Pour water into the tank to the lowest level (mine is level 1, which equals about ⅓ cup water).

Put the berries in the steamer basket or cooking compartment.

Start the cooking process. When the cooking process is done, drain and discard the cooking liquid. Pour the berries and sugar into the blending bowl. Blend very briefly, for only 2 seconds; you just want some of the berries to blend together. Allow it to cool a bit or refrigerate before serving.

To make the parfait, layer the yogurt, berry puree, and granola in a bowl and enjoy.

fillable tank

Fill the water tank with water.

Place the berries in the blending bowl.

Set the steam timer for 5 minutes. When the cooking process is done, drain and discard the cooking liquid. Add the sugar to the blending bowl and blend very briefly, for only 2 seconds; you just want some of the berries to blend. Allow it to cool a bit or refrigerate before serving.

To make the parfait, layer the yogurt, berry puree, and granola in a bowl and enjoy.

stovetop

In a 2-quart saucepan set over high heat, bring ½ cup water to a boil, about 2 minutes. Add the berries, reduce the heat to medium-low, and place a tight-fitting lid on the saucepan. Steam for about 2 minutes, or until the berries are easily pierced with a fork. Drain and discard the cooking liquid.

Transfer the berries to a blender (or food processor) and add the sugar. Blend very briefly, for only 2 seconds; you just want some of the berries to blend. Allow it to cool a bit or refrigerate before serving.

To make the parfait, layer the yogurt, berry puree, and granola in a bowl and enjoy.

NOTE: Make the berry puree the day or night ahead of time so that it's cooled and ready to enjoy the next morning.

edamame dip

makes 1½ cups

1½ cups fresh or frozen shelled edamame (about 6¼ ounces)

1 garlic clove, sliced

3 tablespoons extra-virgin olive oil

Juice of 1 lime

½ teaspoon ground cumin

¼ teaspoon cayenne pepper

¼ cup chopped fresh cilantro leaves

Pinch of kosher salt

I once had an amazing edamame dip at a restaurant that came with soft pita pieces for dipping, and I could not stop thinking about it! So I re-created it with a bag of frozen edamame, and it has become a favorite! It is so easy to whip up this dip, it can be made ahead of time (after it has cooled, it keeps for a week in the fridge), and it is fantastic hot or cold. Serve with warm pitas, pita chips, or tortilla chips. You can use any leafy green herb in place of cilantro; parsley or green onions are two of my favorite substitutions. And any leftover dip can be used as a sandwich spread!

water level

Pour water into the tank to the highest level (mine is level 3, which equals about 1 cup water).

Put the edamame and garlic in the steamer basket or cooking compartment.

Start the cooking process. When the cooking process is done, drain but reserve the cooking liquid; set it aside. Pour the edamame and garlic into the blending bowl and add the remaining ingredients. Blend until thick and creamy. You may have to scrape down the sides of the bowl a few times; if it's too thick, add some reserved cooking liquid, a teaspoon or two at a time. Serve warm or cold.

fillable tank

Fill the water tank with water.

Place the edamame and garlic in the blending bowl.

Set the steam timer for 15 minutes. When the cooking process is done, drain and reserve the cooking liquid, setting it aside. Add the remaining ingredients to the blending bowl with the edamame and garlic. Blend until thick and creamy. You may have to scrape down the sides of the bowl a few times; if it's too thick, add some reserved cooking liquid, a teaspoon or two at a time. Serve warm or cold.

stovetop

In a small 2-quart saucepan set over high heat, bring 1 cup water (about 1 inch) to a boil, about 3 minutes. Add the edamame and garlic, reduce the heat to medium-low, and place a tight-fitting lid on the saucepan. Steam for about 10 minutes, or until the edamame are easily pierced with a fork.

Drain and reserve the cooking liquid, setting it aside. Transfer the edamame and garlic to a blender (or food processor) with the remaining ingredients. Blend until thick and creamy. You may have to scrape down the sides of the bowl a few times; if it's too thick, add some reserved cooking liquid, a teaspoon or two at a time. Serve warm or cold.

strawberry sauce

makes 2 cups

2 cups hulled and halved strawberries

2 tablespoons sugar

1 teaspoon pure vanilla extract

This strawberry sauce can be used in many ways: as a topping for oatmeal, yogurt, or granola in the morning, over pancakes or waffles in place of syrup, in a smoothie bowl, on top of pound cake, or as an ice cream topping. Whatever way it is used, this is delicious! Ripe strawberries are naturally sweet on their own, but the extra touch of sugar here really takes them to the next level.

water level

Pour water into the tank to the highest level (mine is level 3, which equals about 1 cup water).

Put the strawberries, sugar, and vanilla in the steamer basket or cooking compartment.

Start the cooking process. When the cooking process is done, pour the strawberries into the blending bowl with the cooking liquid and blend until smooth.

fillable tank

Fill the water tank with water.

Place strawberries, sugar, and vanilla in the blending bowl.

Set the steam timer for 15 minutes. When the timer goes off, blend the strawberries with the cooking liquid until smooth.

stovetop

In a 2-quart saucepan set over high heat, bring 1 cup water to a boil, about 3 minutes. Add the strawberries, sugar, and vanilla; reduce the heat to medium-low; and place a tight-fitting lid on the saucepan. Steam for about 10 minutes, stirring occasionally, until the strawberries easily mush when pressed with the back of a spoon.

Transfer the strawberries to a blender (or food processor) with the cooking liquid and blend until smooth.

NOTE: If the strawberry sauce is too thick, add a teaspoon of water at a time until the desired consistency is reached.

lentil
curry

makes 2 cups; serves
2 adults over rice

¼ cup full-fat canned
coconut milk

¼ cup no-sodium vegetable
broth

1 cup peeled and cubed winter
squash or sweet potato

2 tablespoons chopped onion

½ teaspoon curry powder

¼ teaspoon grated fresh ginger

¼ teaspoon garlic salt

Squeeze of fresh lemon juice
(optional)

¼ teaspoon ground coriander
(optional)

⅓ cup cooked brown lentils

Lentils make for such a great curry dish. Here they combine with winter squash for a thick, velvety sauce that can be served either as is or over a bed of brown rice, topped with green onions and fresh cilantro or other herbs like parsley or basil. I like using red, French, or brown lentils, but feel free to use whatever kind you like. Filling, delicious, and the perfect cozy vegetarian dinner, it is so easy to make in the baby food maker!

water level

Pour water into the tank to the highest level (mine is level 3, which equals about 1 cup water).

Pour the coconut milk and broth into the blending bowl. Put the remaining ingredients except the cooked brown lentils in the steamer basket or cooking compartment.

Start the cooking process. When the cooking process is done, pour the contents of the steamer basket into the blending bowl with the cooking liquid. Blend until smooth.

Stir in the cooked lentils so that the sauce coats them, and serve.

fillable tank

Fill the water tank with water.

Pour the coconut milk and vegetable broth into the blending bowl and add the remaining ingredients, except the cooked brown lentils.

Set the steam timer for 25 minutes. When the timer goes off, blend the contents of the blending bowl with the cooking liquid until smooth. Stir in the cooked lentils so that the sauce coats them, and serve.

stovetop

In a 2-quart saucepan set over high heat, bring ¾ cup water to a boil, about 3 minutes. Add all the ingredients, except the brown lentils, reduce the heat to medium-low, and place a tight-fitting lid on the saucepan. Steam for 10 to 12 minutes, or until the squash cubes are easily pierced with a fork.

Transfer the contents of the saucepan to a blender (or food processor) with the cooking liquid and blend until smooth. Stir in the cooked red lentils so that the sauce coats them, and serve.

mango pear chutney

makes 2 cups

2 mangoes, peeled, pitted, and cut into slices, or 1½ cups frozen mango pieces

½ ripe medium pear, peeled, cored, and cut into slices

1 tablespoon finely chopped red onion

1 tablespoon raisins, preferably golden

1 tablespoon white vinegar

1 tablespoon sugar

½ teaspoon grated fresh ginger

¼ teaspoon crushed red pepper flakes

Mango and pear chutney is the perfect condiment to accompany meat (chicken, pork, or lamb), to serve alongside a cheese plate, or to smear on bread before making a grilled cheese. This chutney is super simple to make and is sweet with a nice bit of heat in it.

water level

Pour water into the tank to the lowest level (mine is level 1, which equals about ⅓ cup water).

Place all the ingredients in the steamer basket or cooking compartment.

Start the cooking process. When the cooking process is done, drain and discard a little (about 1 tablespoon) of the cooking liquid. Pour the ingredients into the blending bowl with the remaining cooking liquid. Blend very briefly, only 15 to 20 seconds; you want some chunks to remain. Allow it to cool before serving, and store any leftovers in the refrigerator in an airtight container for up to 2 weeks.

fillable tank

Fill the water tank with water.

Place all the ingredients in the blending bowl.

Set the steam timer for 5 minutes. When the cooking process is done, drain and discard a little (about 1 tablespoon) of the cooking liquid.

Blend very briefly, 15 to 20 seconds; you want some chunks to remain. Allow it to cool before serving, and store any leftovers in the refrigerator in an airtight container for up to 2 weeks.

stovetop

In a 2-quart saucepan set over high heat, bring ½ cup water to a boil, about 2 minutes. Add all the ingredients, reduce the heat to medium-low, and place a tight-fitting lid on the saucepan. Steam for about 2 minutes, or until the mango slices are easily pierced with a fork. Drain and discard a little (about 1 tablespoon) of the cooking liquid.

Transfer the ingredients to a blender (or food processor) with the remaining cooking liquid. Blend very briefly, only 15 to 20 seconds; you want some chunks to remain. Allow it to cool before serving, and store any leftovers in the refrigerator in an airtight container for up to 2 weeks.

mashed garlic herb potatoes

makes 1 generous cup

1 large russet potato (about 6 ounces), peeled and cut into ½- to ¾-inch cubes

1 garlic clove, quartered or coarsely chopped

¼ cup milk or nondairy milk, such as unsweetened almond milk, plus more as needed

1 tablespoon sour cream

½ tablespoon unsalted butter

Pinch of chopped fresh herbs (I like using parsley, oregano, and rosemary)

Pinch of salt

There's nothing more comforting than perfectly creamy and delicious mashed potatoes with a hint of garlic and herbs. Mashed potatoes are the quintessential side dish. The only problem? I could eat about five servings in the blink of an eye. With these single-serving mashed potatoes, I can whip up a batch with built-in portion control in no time.

water level

Pour water into the tank to the highest level (mine is level 3, which equals about 1 cup water).

Put the potato and garlic in the steamer basket or cooking compartment and pour in the milk as well; it will go through the steamer basket or cooking compartment into the blending bowl (or you could pour the milk directly into the blending bowl before inserting the steamer basket).

Start the cooking process. When the cooking process is done, pour the potato and garlic into the blending bowl with the cooking liquid and milk. Add the remaining ingredients and blend until smooth. If it's too thick, add a teaspoon or more of milk to reach the desired consistency.

fillable tank

Fill the water tank with water.

Place the potato and garlic in the blending bowl and pour the milk into the blending bowl as well.

Set the steam timer for 25 minutes. When the timer goes off, add the remaining ingredients and blend until smooth. If it's too thick, add a teaspoon or more of milk to reach the desired consistency.

stovetop

In a 2-quart saucepan set over high heat, bring ½ cup water to a boil, about 2 minutes. Add the potato, garlic, and milk; reduce the heat to medium-low; and place a tight-fitting lid on the saucepan. Steam for 10 to 12 minutes, or until the potato cubes are easily pierced with a fork.

Transfer the potato and garlic to a blender (or food processor) with the cooking liquid, add the remaining ingredients, and blend until smooth. If it's too thick, add a teaspoon or more of milk to reach the desired consistency.

NOTE: If you don't mind the potato skin in mashed potatoes, feel free to leave it on. I make these mashed potatoes with and without the skins, and both taste great.

mashed
sweet
potatoes

makes 1 to 1½ cups

1 large sweet potato (about 6 ounces), peeled and cut into ½- to ¾-inch cubes (about 2 cups)

¼ cup milk or nondairy milk, such as unsweetened almond milk, plus more as needed

1 tablespoon pure maple syrup

1 tablespoon unsalted butter

¼ teaspoon ground cinnamon

I never thought to make mashed sweet potatoes until I had them at a farm-to-table restaurant, and I fell in love with them. They are a wonderful side next to meat loaf, with a smooth, creamy texture and subtle sweetness. Made as a single serving here, they're great as a side dish that babies, toddlers, and grown-ups alike will love!

water level

Pour water into the tank to the highest level (mine is level 3, which equals about 1 cup water).

Put the sweet potato in the steamer basket or cooking compartment and pour in the milk as well; it will go through the steamer basket or cooking compartment into the blending bowl (or you could pour the milk directly into the blending bowl before inserting the steamer basket).

Start the cooking process. When the cooking process is done, pour the sweet potato into the blending bowl with the cooking liquid and milk. Add the remaining ingredients and blend until smooth. If it's too thick, add a teaspoon or more of milk to reach the desired consistency.

fillable tank

Fill the water tank with water.

Place the sweet potato in the blending bowl and pour the milk into the blending bowl as well.

Set the steam timer for 25 minutes. When the timer goes off, add the remaining ingredients and blend until smooth. If it's too thick, add a teaspoon or more of milk to reach the desired consistency.

stovetop

In a 2-quart saucepan set over high heat, bring ½ cup water to a boil, about 2 minutes. Add the sweet potato and milk, reduce the heat to medium-low, and place a tight-fitting lid on the saucepan. Steam for 10 to 12 minutes, or until the sweet potato cubes are easily pierced with a fork.

Transfer the sweet potato to a blender (or food processor) with the cooking liquid, add the remaining ingredients, and blend until smooth. If it's too thick, add a teaspoon or more of milk to reach the desired consistency.

NOTE: **Looking for a delicious meat loaf recipe to make with these sweet potatoes? Visit sweetphi.com/extras.**

tomato sauce

makes ¾ to 1 cup

3 medium-large tomatoes, cored and quartered (I like vine, Roma, or an heirloom tomato variety for this)

1 tablespoon chopped onion

1 garlic clove, chopped

Generous pinch of kosher salt

1 tablespoon tomato paste

Is there anything better than pasta sauce made with fresh tomatoes in the summertime? I love making this tomato pasta sauce in a baby food maker after I've been to the farmers' market and have fresh, ripe tomatoes to work with. It comes together in a flash, is great over whole-wheat pasta, and is the only pasta sauce you'll see my family eating when tomatoes are in season!

water level

Pour water into the tank to the highest level (mine is level 3, which equals about 1 cup water).

Place all the ingredients except the tomato paste in the steamer basket or cooking compartment.

Start the cooking process. When the cooking process is done, drain and discard the cooking liquid. Pour the contents of the steamer basket into the blending bowl and add the tomato paste. Blend until smooth. If the sauce seems a little too thick, add a few teaspoons of water until the desired consistency is reached.

NOTE: If you have a baby food maker with an open spout, you might want to hold a paper towel or kitchen cloth over the opening when blending so the sauce doesn't spurt out.

fillable tank

Fill the water tank with water.

Place all the ingredients except the tomato paste in the blending bowl.

Set the steam timer for 20 minutes. When the timer goes off, drain and discard the cooking liquid. Add the tomato paste and blend until smooth. If the sauce seems a little too thick, add a few teaspoons of water until the desired consistency is reached.

stovetop

In a 2-quart saucepan set over high heat, bring ½ cup water to a boil, about 2 minutes. Add all the ingredients except the tomato paste, reduce the heat to medium-low, and place a tight-fitting lid on the saucepan. Steam for about 10 minutes, or until the tomato pieces are very tender when pierced with a fork. Drain and discard the cooking liquid.

Transfer the contents of the saucepan to a blender (or food processor), add the tomato paste, and blend until smooth. If the sauce seems a little too thick, add a few teaspoons of water until the desired consistency is reached.

sun-dried tomato spread

makes ⅔ cup

4 sun-dried tomatoes, chopped (about ¼ cup)

½ cup cooked pinto or white beans (cannellini, navy, or Great Northern), drained and rinsed

1 tablespoon chopped onion

1 tablespoon extra-virgin olive oil

1 teaspoon red wine vinegar

¼ teaspoon garlic salt

¼ teaspoon dried oregano

This beautiful red sun-dried tomato spread is great for sandwiches, as a dip, or added to pastas. It is so versatile, and the summery bright flavor of sun-dried tomatoes really comes through. This recipe uses the type of sun-dried tomatoes that look like dried fruit, not the ones that are marinated in oil (and more expensive). In most grocery stores, the dry kind is usually found with the olives and canned tomatoes.

water level

Pour water into the tank to the medium level (mine is level 2, which equals about ⅔ cup water).

Put the sun-dried tomato, beans, and onion in the steamer basket or cooking compartment.

Start the cooking process. When the cooking process is done, drain and discard the cooking liquid and pour the sun-dried tomato, beans, and onion into the blending bowl. Add the remaining ingredients. Blend until smooth.

fillable tank

Fill the water tank with water.

Put the sun-dried tomato, beans, and onion in the blending bowl.

Set the steam timer for 10 minutes. When the timer goes off, drain and discard the cooking liquid. Add the remaining ingredients to the blending bowl. Blend until smooth.

stovetop

In a 2-quart saucepan set over high heat, bring ½ cup water to a boil, about 2 minutes. Add the sun-dried tomato, beans, and onion; reduce the heat to medium-low; and place a tight-fitting lid on the saucepan. Steam for 5 minutes. Drain the cooking liquid.

Transfer the sun-dried tomato, beans, and chopped onion to a blender (or food processor). Add the remaining ingredients and blend until smooth.

white bean and garlic dip

makes 2 cups

1 (15-ounce) can cannellini or Great Northern beans, rinsed and drained

Juice of 1 lemon (about 2 tablespoons)

1 garlic clove, pressed

½ teaspoon dried oregano

½ teaspoon kosher salt

2 tablespoons extra-virgin olive oil

I'm not going to lie. This dip is super addicting! Once you have a bite of the velvety spread with its zippy lemon and garlic flavor, you're going to make it time and time again. What I love about this recipe is that it's a fantastic last-minute dip you can whip up quickly and serve to guests, and it also works as a sandwich spread.

water level

Pour water into the tank to the lowest level (mine is level 1, which equals about ⅓ cup water).

Put the beans in the steamer basket or cooking compartment. Pour the lemon juice on top of the beans and add the garlic, oregano, and salt.

Start the cooking process. When the cooking process is done, drain and discard the cooking liquid and pour the beans into the blending bowl. Add the olive oil and blend until smooth.

fillable tank

Fill the water tank with water.

Put the beans in the blending bowl. Pour the lemon juice on top and add the garlic, oregano, and salt.

Set the steam timer for 5 minutes. When the timer goes off, drain and discard the cooking liquid and add the olive oil to the blending bowl. Blend until smooth.

stovetop

In a 2-quart saucepan set over high heat, bring ½ cup water to a boil, about 2 minutes. Add the beans, lemon juice, garlic, oregano, and salt; reduce the heat to medium-low; and place a tight-fitting lid on the saucepan. Steam for 3 minutes. Drain the cooking liquid.

Transfer the contents of the saucepan to a blender (or food processor), add the olive oil, and blend until smooth.

banana-carrot cake

water level devices with steamer basket only

serves 1

½ ripe medium banana, mashed (see Note)

¼ cup shredded carrot

1 tablespoon maple syrup

¼ teaspoon pure vanilla extract

2 tablespoons whole milk

2 tablespoons whole-wheat flour

1 tablespoon quick-cooking oats

¼ teaspoon baking powder

⅛ teaspoon ground nutmeg or cinnamon

Just like a healthy muffin, this mini banana-carrot cake is the perfect sweet breakfast for you or your little one. A mix between carrot cake and banana bread, this "cakelette" is loaded with perfectly balanced flavors.

In a small bowl, combine all the ingredients and stir to blend well.

Spray a 6-ounce ramekin lightly with cooking spray. Spoon the batter into the ramekin and cover it with plastic wrap so that water doesn't get into the batter. Place the ramekin in the steamer basket.

Pour water into the tank to the highest level (mine is level 3, which equals about 1 cup water).

Place the steamer basket with the ramekin in the blending bowl and start the cooking process. When the cooking process is done, release the lid and wait for a few minutes, then take out the steamer basket and carefully remove the ramekin. It will be hot, so be sure to use hot pads or tongs.

Take off the plastic wrap and then remove the banana-carrot cake from the ramekin. Let it cool before serving.

NOTE: Ripe bananas—the ones with the brown spots on their skins—are what you want to use, because bananas become sweeter as they ripen.

banana bread

water level devices with steamer basket only

serves 1

½ ripe medium banana, mashed (see Note)

½ teaspoon pure vanilla extract

1½ tablespoons whole milk

2 tablespoons whole-wheat flour

1 tablespoon quick-cooking oats

¼ teaspoon baking powder

⅛ teaspoon ground cinnamon

The first time I tested this recipe, I thought I'd give my son a little bite to try. I liked it, but I wanted to see his reaction. He kept reaching for more, so I gave him bite after bite, until he ate the entire mini banana bread! It is super delicious, baby approved, and is a healthy and baby-friendly banana bread recipe. This would make a fantastic after-school snack or breakfast any day of the week.

In a small bowl, combine all the ingredients and stir to blend thoroughly until there is no trace of the dry ingredients.

Spray a 6-ounce ramekin lightly with cooking spray. Spoon the batter into the ramekin and cover it with plastic wrap so that water doesn't get into the batter. Place the ramekin in the steamer basket.

Pour water into the tank to the highest level (mine is level 3, which equals about 1 cup water).

Place the steamer basket with the ramekin in the blending bowl and start the cooking process. When the cooking process is done, release the lid and wait for a few minutes, then remove the steamer basket and carefully lift out the ramekin. It will be hot, so be sure to use hot pads or tongs.

Take off the plastic wrap and then remove the banana bread from the ramekin. Let it cool slightly before serving.

NOTE: Ripe bananas—the ones with the brown spots on their skins—are the ones you want to use, because bananas become sweeter as they ripen.

baby spice cake

water level devices with steamer basket only

serves 1

1 egg yolk

1 tablespoon brown sugar

½ teaspoon pure vanilla extract

3 tablespoons whole milk

3½ tablespoons all-purpose flour

¼ teaspoon baking powder

¼ teaspoon ground allspice

I could not believe how good this baby spice cake was when I first made it. I gave a bite to my husband to try, and he confirmed it: this is delicious! Allspice really adds a bold flavor. This also rises beautifully, so when putting on the plastic wrap before baking, make sure it's on the loose side. This cakelette makes the perfect sweet treat for both you and your baby. If I'm craving something sweet, I'll just whip up a mini spice cake for dessert.

In a small bowl, combine the egg yolk and brown sugar and stir to blend thoroughly. Add the vanilla and milk and stir until combined. Add the flour, baking powder, and allspice and stir until all the ingredients are incorporated.

Spray a 6-ounce ramekin lightly with cooking spray. Spoon the batter into the ramekin and cover it loosely with plastic wrap so that water doesn't get into the batter. Place the ramekin in the steamer basket.

Pour water into the tank to the highest level (mine is level 3, which equals about 1 cup water).

Place the steamer basket with the ramekin into the blending bowl and start the cooking process. When the cooking process is done, release the lid and wait for a few minutes, then take out the steamer basket and carefully remove the ramekin. It will be hot, so be sure to use hot pads or tongs.

Take off the plastic wrap and then remove the baby spice cake from the ramekin. Let it cool before serving.

baby scrambled egg cup
water level devices with steamer basket only

serves 1

1 large egg, beaten

1 teaspoon whole milk

Eating eggs is such a great way to start the day! I like to make these scrambled egg cups for my son, because I can just put them in the baby food maker as I'm doing a million other things to get the day started, and when the timer goes off, I have a delicious scrambled egg to serve!

In a small bowl, whisk the egg and milk together.

Spray a 6-ounce ramekin lightly with cooking spray. Spoon the egg into the ramekin and cover it loosely with plastic wrap so that water doesn't get into the egg; the egg will rise when it finishes cooking, so give it a little room to rise. Place the ramekin in the steamer basket.

Pour water into the tank to the highest level (mine is level 3, which equals about 1 cup water).

Place the steamer basket with the ramekin in the blending bowl and start the cooking process. When the cooking process is done, release the lid and wait a minute; the egg will puff up and then settle down. Take out the steamer basket and carefully remove the ramekin; it will be hot, so be sure to use hot pads or tongs.

Take off the plastic wrap and then remove the egg from the ramekin. Break it up into pieces, let it cool slightly, and serve.

Note: I like adding already steamed vegetables, such as sweet potatoes or carrots, before putting the scrambled egg into the baby food maker. Then, when it is done cooking, I like to add a pinch of shredded Cheddar cheese to make this scrambled egg cup into a faux omelet for baby.

baby vanilla cupcake

water level devices
with steamer
basket only

serves 1

1 egg yolk

1½ tablespoons whole milk

1 tablespoon plain full-fat Greek yogurt

⅛ teaspoon pure almond extract

¼ teaspoon pure vanilla extract

3 tablespoons all-purpose flour

1 tablespoon sugar

¼ teaspoon baking powder

There's something about the smell and taste of vanilla that reminds me of childhood. But this baby vanilla cupcake is suitable for adults too—don't get me wrong. Adding a few drops of almond extract to vanilla really brings out the vanilla flavor in cake, which is why you'll always find it in my vanilla cake recipes.

In a small bowl, combine the egg yolk, milk, yogurt, and both extracts. In another bowl, combine the flour, sugar, and baking powder. Combine the wet and dry ingredients until incorporated and no trace of dry ingredients remains.

Put a paper cupcake liner, if desired, into a 6-ounce ramekin and spray it lightly with cooking spray (this step is optional; you could spray the ramekin itself instead of using a liner). Spoon the batter into the ramekin and cover it loosely with plastic wrap so that water doesn't get into the batter. Place the ramekin in the steamer basket.

Pour water into the tank to the highest level (mine is level 3, which equals about 1 cup water).

Place the steamer basket with the ramekin in the blending bowl and start the cooking process. When the cooking process is done, release the lid and wait for a few minutes, then take out the steamer basket and carefully remove the ramekin; it will be hot, so be sure to use hot pads or tongs.

Take off the plastic wrap and then remove the vanilla cupcake from the ramekin. Let it cool before serving.

chocolate cakelette

water level devices with steamer basket only

serves 1

¼ cup semisweet chocolate chips

1 tablespoon unsalted butter

1 tablespoon sugar

1 egg yolk

2½ tablespoons all-purpose flour

We all need a little chocolate fix every once in a while. This single-serving chocolate cakelette is perfect for those chocolate cravings. And the best part is that if you are feeling nice, you can share a bite with your baby and not feel bad about giving something too sweet. It's rich and chocolaty perfection.

In a small microwave-safe bowl, combine the chocolate chips and butter. Microwave on high for 30 seconds. Remove the bowl from the microwave and stir; return to the microwave for an additional 30 seconds, or until the chocolate and butter are completely melted.

Add the sugar and stir until incorporated, then add the egg yolk and flour and stir until combined.

Spray a 6-ounce ramekin lightly with cooking spray. Spoon the batter into the ramekin and cover it loosely with plastic wrap so that water doesn't get into the batter. Place the ramekin in the steamer basket.

Pour water into the tank to the highest level (mine is level 3, which equals about 1 cup water).

Place the steamer basket with the ramekin in the blending bowl and start the cooking process. When the cooking process is done, release the lid and wait for a few minutes, then take out the steamer basket and carefully remove the ramekin; it will be hot, so be sure to use hot pads or tongs.

Take off the plastic wrap and then remove the chocolate cake from the ramekin. Let it cool slightly before serving.

the top 12 ways to use your baby food maker after baby food

Even though my baby is now over one year old (where does the time go?), I still use my baby food maker all the time. It's perfect for preparing things that use steamed fruit or veggies, and it saves so much time. Here are some of my favorite things to create with the baby food maker once you're done using it solely for baby food (also see Block Five: Beyond Baby for a few ways adults can cook with the baby food maker).

1

batter for pancakes
with steamed vegetables or fruit

Sweet potato pancakes are easy to make with the baby food maker. Just steam sweet potatoes and use the following recipe:

sweet potato pancakes

makes 14 small pancakes

½ cup Sweet Potato Puree (page 32)

2 large eggs, beaten

¾ cup whole milk

1 teaspoon pure vanilla extract

1 cup whole-wheat flour

2 tablespoons sugar

1 teaspoon baking powder

½ teaspoon baking soda

½ teaspoon ground cinnamon

½ teaspoon ground nutmeg

In a medium bowl, stir together the sweet potato puree, eggs, milk, and vanilla. In a separate bowl, combine the whole-wheat flour, sugar, baking powder, baking soda, cinnamon, and nutmeg. Combine the dry and wet ingredients and stir until blended.

Heat a skillet or griddle, spray with cooking spray, and pour the batter to form pancakes; I like to use a 2-tablespoon cookie scoop to make equal-size pancakes. Flip halfway through cooking, about 3 minutes, or when bubbles start to form on the surface and the underside is starting to turn golden brown, and cook about 3 more minutes. Enjoy the pancakes with maple syrup, butter, and/or banana slices on top.

NOTE: You can make many other kinds of fruit or vegetable pancakes. Use the above recipe and swap the puree of your choice for sweet potatoes. For example, you can make savory broccoli pancakes, squash pancakes, or carrot pancakes, replacing the sugar with shredded Cheddar or Parmesan cheese.

2

small-batch marinara sauce

Use the baby food maker to make a small batch of marinara sauce. Follow the recipe for Tomato Sauce on page 199.

3

veggies for unique meatball filling

Cooked sweet potato, ginger, carrot, or cauliflower pieces make great fillings for meatballs. Next time you're making a batch of meatballs, try mixing in some vegetables that have been cooked in your baby food maker, just like the Baby Meatballs with Carrots and Herbs (page 143) or the Savory Apple-Turkey Meatballs (page 170).

4

small-batch
vegetable and cheese sauce

As much as I like those neon-yellow boxed mac 'n' cheese packages, I prefer to eat a more balanced cheesy sauce, and I achieve that by mixing in vegetables. Carrots or butternut squash makes a great addition to cheese sauce because their orange colors make the sauce look extra cheesy. See the Secretly Carrot Cheddar Cheese Sauce on page 155. I also make Alfredo Sauce with Cauliflower (below).

alfredo sauce with cauliflower

make 2 cups sauce

1 tablespoon unsalted butter

½ teaspoon garlic salt

¼ cup grated Parmesan cheese

⅓ cup whole milk

¼ cup plain full-fat yogurt

Prepare a batch of Cauliflower Puree (page 36) but before blending, add the butter, garlic salt, cheese, milk, and yogurt. Blend until smooth and enjoy—it's so good over pasta!

5

soups for lunches

Craving a cup of soup? With your baby food maker, single-serving soup is super easy and quick. Try the following recipes for a delicious soup:

White Fish Chowder (page 153)

Potato Leek Soup (page 168)

Basil, Tomato, and Winter Squash Soup (page 173— my personal favorite to serve alongside a grilled cheese)

Tuscan White Bean Soup (page 177)

6

dips

Dips are my favorite part of parties. Anyone else? Here are a few dip recipes I love making:

Chickpea–Sweet Potato Spread (page 187)

Edamame Dip (page 189)

Sun-Dried Tomato Spread (page 200)

White Bean and Garlic Dip (page 202)

7

veggie and fish burgers, fritters, and nuggets

Making a batter that would normally need multiple pots is a breeze with a baby food maker. Simply steam the veggies and/or protein, combine it with the other ingredients, and turn it into burgers, fritters, or nuggets that are fried on the stovetop or baked in the oven.

salmon burgers

makes 4 mini salmon burgers

2 ounces deboned salmon, skin removed, cut into cubes

½ cup peeled and cubed sweet potato

¼ medium bell pepper, seeded, ribs removed, and cut into small pieces (about ¼ cup)

¼ cup bread crumbs, or 2 tablespoons whole-wheat flour

1 egg yolk

Pinch of garlic powder

Pinch of dried parsley and/or dill

Preheat the oven to 350°F.

Steam the salmon, sweet potato, and bell pepper in your baby food maker (level 3, or timer set to 25 minutes). Drain the cooking liquid and add the remaining ingredients to the blending bowl.

Blend until combined.

Spray a baking sheet with cooking spray.

Form the mixture into 4 small burger patties using a spoon or your hands and place them on the baking sheet. Bake for 10 minutes.

Alternatively, add a dash of extra-virgin olive oil or spray a nonstick skillet with cooking spray and sauté the patties over high heat for 3 minutes, then flip and cook them for another 3 minutes.

NOTE: **You can make these burgers using a different protein in place of the salmon: chicken, beef, lamb, tofu, or chickpeas.**

broccoli or cauliflower nuggets

makes 15 to 20 nuggets

2 cups broccoli or cauliflower florets

½ cup bread crumbs

1 egg

2 tablespoons whole milk

¼ cup shredded Cheddar cheese

¼ teaspoon garlic powder

Preheat the oven to 375°F.

Cook the florets in your baby food maker (level 3, or timer set to 20 minutes). Drain the cooking liquid and add the remaining ingredients to the blending bowl. Blend until combined.

Spray a baking sheet with cooking spray.

Form small nuggets using a 1-tablespoon scoop or your hands and place them about 1 inch apart on the baking sheet. Bake for about 20 minutes, or until the edges turn golden brown.

Alternatively, add a dash of extra-virgin olive oil or spray a nonstick skillet with cooking spray and sauté the nuggets over high heat for about 5 minutes, or until the edges turn golden brown, then flip and cook for about another 5 minutes. You might need a little bit more olive oil to prevent them from sticking in the skillet.

veggies for baked egg cups

Baked egg cups packed with veggies are such a great breakfast, and because they reheat so well, they are great for meal prep (make a batch on Sunday for the week ahead).

baked egg cups

makes 6 muffins

¼ cup peeled and cubed sweet potato

¼ cup peeled and chopped carrot

¼ cup chopped bell pepper

¼ cup chopped baby spinach (optional)

4 large eggs, beaten

⅓ cup shredded Cheddar cheese

2 tablespoons whole milk

2 tablespoons whole milk ricotta cheese

Steam the sweet potato, carrot, and bell pepper in your baby food maker (level 3, or timer set to 20 minutes). Drain the cooking liquid and let the veggies cool for 10 minutes.

Preheat the oven to 350°F. Line a muffin tin with 6 liners (or line a mini muffin tin with 12 mini liners) or spray the cups with nonstick cooking spray.

In a small bowl, combine the eggs, cheese, milk, and ricotta and blend together. Stir in the cooked veggies and chopped spinach (if using) and spoon the batter evenly into the lined muffin tin.

Bake for about 20 minutes, or until the edges just start to turn golden brown; they will deflate a little as they cool. Serve and enjoy!

9

fruit spreads
for jam crumb bars

I love making jam crumb bars. They're a super simple dessert for
feeding a crowd because the recipe makes a sheet pan of bars, easily
32 servings or more. This recipe is adapted from my first cookbook,
Fast and Easy Five-Ingredient Recipes: A Cookbook for Busy People. It's
always a crowd-pleaser! I now use my baby food maker to make
the jam filling; I usually like to use raspberries or a combination like
blueberries, strawberries, and raspberries. I love how that really takes
the recipe to the next level, because everything is homemade!

jam crumb bars

makes 32 bars

2 cups berries or chopped fruit
(your choice)

1 cup plus 1 tablespoon sugar

1 teaspoon pure vanilla extract

1½ cups (3 sticks) unsalted
butter

2 cups all-purpose flour

1 cup rolled oats

Make a berry or fruit puree in
your baby food maker: Combine
the fruit, the 1 tablespoon sugar,
and the vanilla in your baby
food maker (level 1, or timer set
to 5 minutes). Drain a little of the
cooking liquid and then blend
the berries with the remaining
cooking liquid until smooth. Allow
it to cool slightly; this puree can
be made ahead of time.

Preheat the oven to 375°F. Use
a little of the butter to grease a
10 × 15 × 1–inch jelly-roll pan.

Cut 1 cup (2 sticks) of the butter
into pieces and place it in a food
processor. Add 1⅔ cups of the
flour, ⅔ cup of the sugar, and
⅓ cup of the oats and process on
high speed until combined into a
mealy mixture, about 15 seconds.

Pour the mixture onto the
prepared jelly-roll pan and press
the crumbs down to form an even
crust.

Spread the jam evenly over the
crust.

In the food processor, combine
the remaining (scant) ½ cup
butter, ⅓ cup flour, ⅓ cup sugar,
and ⅔ cup oats and process on
high speed until combined, about
10 seconds, then sprinkle the
mixture evenly over the jam layer.

Bake for about 25 minutes, or
until the edges are golden brown.
Remove from the oven and allow
to cool completely in the pan
before cutting it into squares. I
run a knife around the edges and
then cut 32 squares (see Note),
but you could definitely cut them
into smaller squares to feed an
even bigger crowd.

NOTE: I use a pizza cutter to cut
the bars; it works like a charm.

10

smoothies

You know what can be made with frozen puree cubes? Smoothies! That's right—fruit and vegetable purees lend themselves so well to being made into cool and refreshing drinks. When blending a smoothie, I recommend using a high-power blender.

To make a smoothie, simply make a puree as stated in the appropriate recipe and freeze it in ice-cubes trays until solid. When you're ready to enjoy a smoothie, simply blend the cubes with 1¾ to 2 cups of liquid (I like using unflavored almond milk).

The ratio for two 10- to 15-ounce servings of smoothies is 2 cups of puree turned into ice cubes with 1¾ to 2 cups liquid.

Here are a few purees that make really great smoothies:

- Berry, Date, and Chia Seed Puree (page 108)
- Nectarine, Peach, and Sweet Potato Puree (page 84)
- Apple, Beet, and Strawberry Puree (page 56)
- Blueberry, Melon, and Pear Puree (page 72)
- Mango, Pineapple, and Pumpkin Puree (page 83)
- Banana, Mango, Pear, and Coconut Milk Puree (page 130)
- Berry, Avocado, and Coconut Milk Puree (page 133)
- Mango, Banana, Cauliflower, and Spinach Puree (page 131)
- Banana, Berry, and Grain Puree (page 97)

11

ice pops

You can make some pretty awesome ice pops using your baby food maker. After making the puree, pour it into ice-pop molds and freeze it until solid, about 3 hours—it's that simple! As a general rule, 1 cup puree yields 2 to 2½ ice pops, so using these recipes, I usually get 4 or 5.

For ice-pop recipes, try the following:

- Beet, Apple, and Watermelon Puree (page 134)
- Peach, Nectarine, and Mango Puree page 135)
- Pineapple, Sweet Potato, and Ginger Puree (page 132)

ice cream

Have you ever heard of no-churn ice cream? It's ice cream that doesn't involve an ice cream maker—I'd call that a win! All you need is sweetened condensed milk, heavy cream, and any desired mix-ins. You stir everything together and then pour it into a freezer-safe dish, and in 4 to 5 hours— voilà, you have yourself some ice cream! A loaf pan works well for freezing the ice cream.

no-churn berry ice cream

makes 4 cups

2 cups berries and/or chopped fruit (I like a combination of blueberries, raspberries, and strawberries)

2 cups cold heavy whipping cream

1 (14-ounce) can sweetened condensed milk

Cook the fruit in your baby food maker (level 1, or timer set to 10 minutes). Drain the cooking liquid and blend the fruit into a puree. Let it cool for 10 minutes.

In a large bowl, whip the cream using a hand mixer until soft peaks form (be careful not to overwhip it). Pour in the sweetened condensed milk and fruit puree and blend with the hand mixer until thoroughly combined.

Pour the mixture into a freezer-safe container, cover with plastic wrap or a lid, and put it into the freezer for 4 to 5 hours, until firm and frozen. Scoop and enjoy!

appendix:
cooking-time guide

Here is the cooking-time guide by ingredient. If you're combining ingredients, use the longest cook time.

fruit/vegetable name	water level baby food maker	fillable tank baby food maker	stovetop
Apple	3 (25 mins)	20 mins	10 mins
Apricot	1 (10 mins)	5 mins	2 mins
Asparagus	2 (17 mins)	10 mins	5 mins
Avocado	1 (10 mins)	5 mins	2 mins
Banana	1 (10 mins)	5 mins	2 mins
Beef (ground)	3 (25 mins)	20 mins	10 mins
Beet	3 (25 mins)	25 mins	12 mins
Bell Pepper	3 (25 mins)	20 mins	10 mins
Blueberries	1 (10 mins)	5 mins	2 mins
Broccoli	3 (25 mins)	20 mins	10 mins
Cantaloupe	1 (10 mins)	5 mins	2 mins
Carrot	3 (25 mins)	25 mins	12 mins
Cauliflower	3 (25 mins)	20 mins	10 mins
Cherries	1 (10 mins)	5 mins	2 mins
Corn	2 (17 mins)	10 mins	5 mins
Edamame	3 (25 mins)	15 mins	10 mins
Green Beans	3 (25 mins)	15 mins	10 mins
Kiwi	1 (10 mins)	5 mins	2 mins

fruit/vegetable name	water level baby food maker	fillable tank baby food maker	stovetop
Leafy Greens (spinach or kale)	2 (17 mins)	10 mins	2 mins
Mango	1 (10 mins)	5 mins	2 mins
Nectarine	1 (10 mins)	5 mins	2 mins
Parsnip	3 (25 mins)	25 mins	10 mins
Peach	1 (10 mins)	5 mins	2 mins
Pear	1 (10 mins)	5 mins	2 mins
Peas	2 (17 mins)	10 mins	5 mins
Plum	2 (17 mins)	10 mins	5 mins
Pork	3 (25 mins)	20 mins	10 mins
Potato	3 (25 mins)	25 mins	12 mins
Poultry (chicken)	3 (25 mins)	25 mins	12 mins
Pumpkin	3 (25 mins)	25 mins	12 mins
Seafood	3 (25 mins)	17 mins	25 mins
Strawberries	1 (10 mins)	5 mins	2 mins
Sweet Potato	3 (25 mins)	25 mins	12 mins
Turkey (ground)	3 (25 mins)	25 mins	12 mins
Winter Squash (butternut or acorn squash)	3 (25 mins)	25 mins	12 mins
Zucchini	2 (17 mins)	15 mins	5 mins

acknowledgments

When one picks up a book, one sees an author's name on it and thinks of the author and book as singular. That is, thankfully, not the case. There are so many people behind this book, and for that I am truly grateful.

I'm always at a loss for words to thank my husband. But really, he deserves all the special thank-yous in the world. I love you so much, Nick. You are the reason I am a mom, and for that I am forever grateful. I love our little family. Your constant, unwavering love and support never go unappreciated. I love that you know my "five more minutes of work" really means an hour—at least. I love that you let me take over the dining room, rendering it unusable for anything except as a holding area for my millions of props and photography stuff when I'm working on a big project. You're the best sounding board, and I value your input so much. You always push me to go for my dreams. You make me so happy, and I love you more and more with each day that goes by.

Lynn, thank you for being the most loyal and caring friend a girl could ask for. I hope everyone gets to experience a friendship like ours in their lifetime. I love you—your quick wit and jokes make me laugh endlessly. I love that we're both moms and get to share motherhood stories now!

I could not have done this book without your help, Bridget. You carted endless neutral shirts to our photoshoot days, and you have perfected the art of chopping vegetables—I will be forever grateful for your friendship! Thank you for being the best hand model and cheerleader always helping to get things done.

To my agent, Sally Ekus, thank you for "getting it" and me. I wrote my first cookbook without you, and I'm secretly sad about that because having you in my corner is invaluable. You always push me to really think about an idea or proposal, and your urging me to "take the weekend" to think if I really wanted to work on this project changed my life. I begrudgingly bought a baby food maker thinking I'd hate it. But oh, my goodness, it was one of the best purchases I have ever made; I use it daily to make food for my baby and our family. Thank you for always giving great feedback and steering me in the right direction.

To my editor, Donna Loffredo, you are a wordsmith, and your ideas are amazing. Thank you for shaping this book and steering me in the right direction. I feel as if I responded "Yes, love this idea" to every one of your notes, because you truly took my work to the next level.

Thank you to the best art director, Stephanie Huntwork. Your work is stunning, and I cannot wait to show off this beautiful book; it's a true work of art because of you. Thank you for your comments and attention to the details.

To the entire team at Crown, thank you for turning this book into what it is. It has been such an amazing experience working with all of you.

To all my family and friends, thank you for your continuous support and encouragement. I love and appreciate you all.

Last, but certainly not least, I want to thank all of you for buying this cookbook! I hope your journey of making baby food is made easier as a result of it. I'd like to stay in touch—you can find me at sweetphi.com, and I love seeing your creations using #sweetphiblog on social media.

index

Note: Page references in *italics*
    indicate photographs.

Allergies, 20
Apple
    Beet, and Cherry Puree, 53
    Beet, and Strawberry Puree, 56
    Beet, and Watermelon Puree,
      134
    and Beet Puree, *54,* 55
    Broccoli, and Kale Puree, 58, *59*
    Broccoli, and Pea Puree, 57
    Cinnamon, Raisin, and
      Quinoa Puree, *104,* 105
    Corn, and Sweet Potato
      Puree, 60
    Kiwi, and Spinach Puree, 61
    Pear, and Cinnamon Puree, 94
    -Pear-Cinnamon Sauce, Yo-
      gurt Parfaits with, *182,* 183
    Pumpkin, and Nutmeg Puree,
      96
    Puree, 31
Apricot
    Spinach, Zucchini, and Brown
      Rice Puree, 100, *101*
    Winter Squash, and Banana
      Puree, 62
Asparagus
    Avocado, and Mango Puree,
      64, 65
    Pesto, 181
    Zucchini, and Green Beans,
      Lemony, *166,* 166–67
Avocado
    and Cherry Puree, 63
    Puree, 48, *49*

Baby food
    buying ingredients, 15, 16
    cooking time guide, 220–21
    dos and don'ts, 22
    feeding readiness guidelines,
      15–17

feeding tips, 17–18
food introduction calendar,
    24–27
helpful tools, 22–23
ingredient substitutes, 20
trying new foods, 21–22
Baby food makers, 14–15
Banana
    Berry, and Grain Puree, 97
    Bread, *204, 205*
    -Carrot Cake, 203
    Mango, Pear, and Coconut
      Milk Puree, 130
    Oat, Sweet Potato, and
      Allspice Puree, 110
    Puree, 42
Bars, Jam Crumb, 217
Bean(s). *See also* Green Bean
    Chickpea–Sweet Potato
      Spread, *186,* 187
    Edamame Dip, 189
    Gentle Baby Chili, 159
    Sun-Dried Tomato Spread,
      200, *201*
    White, and Garlic Dip, 202
    White, Soup, Tuscan, *176,* 177
Beef
    Avocado, and Black Bean
      Puree, 116, *117*
    Baby Bolognese, 144, *145*
    and Broccoli with Grain,
      146, 147
    Gentle Baby Chili, 159
    Ground, Peas, and Potatoes, 162
Beet
    Apple, and Watermelon
      Puree, 134
    and Apple Puree, *54,* 55
    Squash, and Yogurt Puree, 111
Berry(ies)
    Avocado, and Coconut Milk
      Puree, 133, *133*
    Banana, and Grain Puree, 97

Blueberry, Melon, and Pear
    Puree, 72, *73*
Crumble, Cheaters', 184, *185*
Date, and Chia Seed Puree,
    108, *109*
Eggplant, and Grain Puree, 114
Granola Parfait, 188
Ice Cream, No-Churn, 219, *219*
Jam Crumb Bars, 217
Quinoa, and Yogurt Puree, 115
and Squash Puree, *70,* 71
Strawberry Sauce, 190, *191*
and Sweet Potato Puree,
    68, *69*
Blueberry, Melon, and Pear
    Puree, 72, *73*
Bread, Banana, *204, 205*
Broccoli
    and Beef with Grain, *146,* 147
    Chicken, and Cheese, 149
    Mango, and Zucchini Puree, 74
    Nuggets, 215
    Puree, 45
    "Rice" and Cheddar, 148
    Teriyaki Salmon, and Brown
      Rice, 158
Burgers, Salmon, 215
Cakes
    Baby Spice, 206
    Baby Vanilla Cupcake, *208,*
      209
    Banana-Carrot, 203
    Chocolate Cakelette, 210, *211*
Carrot(s)
    -Banana Cake, 203
    Cheddar Cheese Sauce,
      Secretly, 155, *155*
    Orange, Nutmeg, and Ginger
      Puree, 98
    Peach, and Pumpkin Puree,
      75
    Pear, and Sweet Potato
      Puree, *76,* 77
    Puree, *34,* 35

and Sweet Potatoes, Indi-
    an-Spiced, 163
Cauliflower
    Alfredo Sauce with, 214
    Nuggets, 215
    Plum, and Date Puree, 78
    Puree, 36
    "Rice," Cilantro Lime, 156, *157*
    Tofu, and Cheese, 150, *151*
Cheese
    Baked Egg Cups, 216
    Broccoli "Rice" and Cheddar,
      148
    Cheddar, Sauce, Secretly
      Carrot, 155, *155*
Chicken
    Apple, and Potatoes, Slightly
      Balsamic, 171
    Baby Barbecue, and Sweet
      Potatoes, 140–41, *141*
    Broccoli, and Cheese, 149
    Ginger-Tomato, and Sweet
      Potatoes, 154
    Kale, and Quinoa Puree, 120
    Lemony Quinoa, 164
    Pea, and Pear Puree, 121
    and Potatoes, Turmeric,
      174, *175*
    Squash, and Potato Puree,
      118, 119
    Sweet Potatoes, and Cumin, 152
Chili, Gentle Baby, 159
Chocolate Cakelette, 210, *211*
Chowder, White Fish, 153
Chutney, Mango Pear, 194, *195*
Corn, Pear, and Cauliflower
    Puree, 79
Cupcake, Baby Vanilla, *208,*
    209
Curry, Lentil, *192,* 193
Dips
    Edamame, 189
    White Bean and Garlic, 202

Egg Cups
    Baby Scrambled, 207, *207*
    Baked, 216
Eggplant, Berry, and Grain
    Puree, 114

Fish. *See also* Salmon
    Garlic, and Cauliflower
        Puree, 124
    purees, introducing, 87
    White, Chowder, 153
Fruit. *See also* specific fruits
    Jam Crumb Bars, 217
    No-Churn Berry Ice Cream,
        219, *219*

Grain(s)
    Baby "Cereals" and, 86
    Berry, and Banana Puree,
        97
Granola Berry Parfait, 188
Green Bean
    Kale, and Pea Puree, 80, *81*
    and Squash Puree, 82

Herbs, 21

Ice Cream, No-Churn Berry,
    219, *219*
Ice Pops, 218

Jam Crumb Bars, 217

Kale Puree, 43

Lentil
    Curry, *192, 193*
    Pepper, and Sweet Potato
        Puree, 129

Mango
    Banana, Cauliflower, and
        Spinach Puree, 131
    Banana, Pear, and Coconut
        Milk Puree, 130
    Pear Chutney, 194, *195*
    Pineapple, and Pumpkin
        Puree, 83
    Pumpkin, and Turmeric
        Puree, 99
    Puree, 44
Meat. *See also* Beef; Pork
    purees, introducing, 87
Meatballs
    Baby, with Carrots and Herbs,
        142, 143
    Savory Apple-Turkey, 170

Nectarine, Peach, and Sweet
    Potato Puree, 84

Pancakes, Sweet Potato, 213
Parsnip
    Beet, and Sweet Potato
        Puree, 66
    Onion, Squash, and Coconut
        Milk Puree, 106
Pea
    Puree, 41
    Spinach, and Basil Puree, 95
Peach
    Nectarine, and Mango Puree,
        135
    Plum, Pepper, and Grain
        Puree, *112, 113*
Pear
    Apple, and Cinnamon Puree,
        94
    -Apple-Cinnamon Sauce, Yo-
        gurt Parfaits with, *182,* 183
    Banana, Mango, and
        Coconut Milk Puree, 130
    Mango Chutney, 194, *195*
    Puree, 40
Pepper, Bell, and Sweet Potato
    Puree, 67
Pesto, Asparagus, 181
Pineapple, Sweet Potato, and
    Ginger Puree, 132
Plum
    Peach, Pepper, and Grain
        Puree, *112, 113*
    Puree, *46, 47*
Pork, Sweet Potato, and Apple
    Puree, 122
Potato(es). *See also* Sweet
        Potato(es)
    and Chicken, Turmeric, 174,
        175
    Ground Beef, and Peas, 162
    Leek Soup, 168, *169*
    Mashed Garlic Herb, 196
    and Salmon, Herby, 160–61,
        161
Poultry. *See also* Chicken; Turkey
    purees, introducing, 87
Pumpkin
    Apple, and Nutmeg Puree, 96
    Mango, and Turmeric Puree, 99
    Puree, *38, 39*
Purees
    chunky, list of, 90
    combination, list of, 52
    making and freezing, 18–19
    single ingredient, list of, 30

transitioning to solids, 19–20

Quinoa Chicken, Lemony, 164

Salmon
    Apricot, and Sweet Potatoes,
        165
    Burgers, 215
    and Potatoes, Herby, 160–61,
        161
    Sweet Potato, and Apple
        Puree, 123
    Teriyaki, Broccoli, and Brown
        Rice, 158
Sauces
    Alfredo, with Cauliflower, 214
    Secretly Carrot Cheddar
        Cheese, 155, *155*
    Strawberry, 190, *191*
    Tomato, *198,* 199
Shrimp Scampi, Baby, 139
Smoothies, 218
Soups
    Basil, Tomato, and Winter
        Squash, 172, *173*
    Potato Leek, 168, *169*
    White Bean, Tuscan, 176, 177
Spice Cake, Baby, 206
Spices, 21
Spinach
    Pea, and Basil Puree, 95
    Puree, 43
    Zucchini, Quinoa, and Cumin
        Puree, 102
Spreads
    Chickpea–Sweet Potato,
        186, 187
    Sun-Dried Tomato, 200, *201*
Squash. *See also* Pumpkin;
        Zucchini
    Beet, and Yogurt Puree, 111
    Butternut or Acorn, Puree, 37
    Lentil Curry, *192, 193*
    Sweet Potato, and Cinnamon
        Puree, *92, 93*
    Winter, Basil, and Tomato
        Soup, 172, *173*
    Winter and Summer, Puree, 85
Strawberry Sauce, 190, *191*
Sweet Potato(es)
    and Baby Barbecue Chicken,
        140–41, *141*
    and Carrots, Indian-Spiced, 163
    Chicken, and Cumin, 152
    –Chickpea Spread, *186,* 187
    Coconut Milk, and Curry
        Puree, 91

and Ginger-Tomato Chicken,
    154
    Mashed, 197
    Oat, Banana, and Allspice
        Puree, 110
    Pancakes, 213
    Pineapple, and Ginger Puree,
        132
    Puree, 32, *33*
    Raisin, Cinnamon, and
        Quinoa Puree, 103
    Salmon, and Apricot, 165
    Squash, and Cinnamon
        Puree, *92, 93*
    Swiss Chard, Beet, Mango, and
        Cinnamon Puree, 107

Tofu
    Carrot, and Cauliflower
        Puree, 125
    Cauliflower, and Cheese,
        150, *151*
    Squash, and Green Bean
        Puree, 126, *127*
    Sweet Potato, and Turmeric
        Puree, 128
Tomato(es)
    Baby Bolognese, 144, *145*
    Basil, and Winter Squash
        Soup, 172, *173*
    Sauce, *198,* 199
    Sun-Dried, Spread, 200, *201*
Turkey
    -Apple Meatballs, Savory, 170
    Baby Meatballs with Carrots
        and Herbs, *142,* 143

Watermelon, Beet, and Apple
    Puree, 134

Yogurt Parfaits with Apple-
    Pear-Cinnamon Sauce,
    182, 183

Zucchini
    Apricot, Spinach, and Brown
        Rice Puree, 100, *101*
    Asparagus, and Green Beans,
        Lemony, *166,* 166–67
    Spinach, Quinoa, and Cumin
        Puree, 102